LOSING MY RELIGION?

Also by Gordon Lynch

After Religion: 'Generation X' and the search for meaning

LOSING MY RELIGION?

Moving on from Evangelical faith

GORDON LYNCH

First published in 2003 by
Darton, Longman and Todd Ltd
1 Spencer Court
140–142 Wandsworth High Street
London SW18 4JJ

© 2003 Gordon Lynch

The right of Gordon Lynch to be identified as the Author
of this work has been asserted in accordance with the
Copyright, Designs and Patents Act 1988.

ISBN 0–232–52505–6

A catalogue record for this book is available from the British Library.

Extract from the song on p. 8: Adm. by
worshiptogether.com songs excl. UK &
Europe, adm. by Kingsway Music.
tym@kingsway.co.uk. Used by permission.

Designed by Sandie Boccacci
Phototypeset in 10/13pt Palatino by Intype Libra Ltd
Printed and bound in Great Britain by
The Bath Press, Bath

*For Tim, Derek and John
with my best wishes to you
on your different journeys*

CONTENTS

INTRODUCTION

As this is the part of a book that many people skip over, I won't get into too many different issues here. I do want to explain a bit about why I have written this book, though. As will be clear from the following chapters (and to anyone who has read my related book, *After Religion: 'Generation X' and the search for meaning*, Darton, Longman and Todd, 2002), I have in the past been a committed Evangelical Christian. Quite how I'd define my spiritual or religious affiliations now is less straightforward, though however I choose to define it, my involvement in the Christian tradition has been very formative on me.

This book is borne partly out of my own experience of moving away from Evangelical faith and from involvement in Evangelical churches. This process was a long one for me – how long depends on quite how I tell the story, but to say that this has been a slow process that has evolved over the past ten or so years would not be stretching the truth. This process has at times been confusing, exciting, liberating and painful, and has certainly been one of the 'big' stories of my life to date. The immediate impetus for writing this book, however, came from attending a seminar at Greenbelt 2002 led by Cole Moreton on 'The Curse of Faith'. This talk, which I say a bit more about later in chapter four, was a profoundly honest account of the shadow-side of an Evangelical faith and lifestyle. What moved me was not only the honesty of this talk, which resonated very much with my own experience, but my realisation that I was sitting in a large conference room crowded out with people who shared similar experiences, questions and doubts. For someone who at times feels odd for having had an Evangelical background and then feels more odd for not even fitting in with that anymore, it was genuinely helpful to realise that my experience was not as strange and unique as I sometimes imagine it to be.

Soon after attending that session, I decided to write this book.

I wanted to do this not because I feel I have anything to offer by way of conclusive answers to the kinds of issues and doubts that people may have when they are questioning their Evangelical beliefs. But rather I feel that my own experience of moving away from Evangelical faith has given me a particular framework for understanding this process. If you do find yourself moving on from Evangelical faith, then this book isn't intended to solve all your questions or searchings but to offer one way of understanding what you might be going through. Having that kind of understanding won't protect you from doubts, uncertainty or pain but may give you some way of containing those feelings and make them less bewildering or overwhelming.

I have deliberately written this book in a way that I hope will be helpful for people who are already engaged in a serious process of questioning or moving away from their Evangelical beliefs. In many ways, I hope that it will also be read by people who are happy with their Evangelical faith but whose partners, close friends or other fellow church members are going through this kind of process. If there is a greater degree of understanding of what people are thinking and feeling when they begin to shift their roots away from Evangelical Christianity, then there may be better prospects that Evangelical churches can offer them appropriate spiritual and pastoral support in the midst of this.

Before we move on to the main text, I need to express my thanks to a number of people. As ever, working with DLT on this book has been very enjoyable and my thanks go to Virginia Hearn for her support and encouragement on this text, as well as to everyone else at DLT who has helped in its production. I am grateful too to various people whose work on Evangelicalism and post-Evangelicalism has shaped my own thinking, in particular to Jo Ind, Alan Jamieson, Cole Moreton and Dave Tomlinson. I'm delighted that I've been able to include interviews with Jo and Dave as part of this book and want to thank them for helping this project with their time and their reflections. Conversations with Robert Beckford have been very helpful in making me think about the kind of theological language that I use. Spending time at some events run by the B1 Church in Birmingham whilst writing this book has also been an encouraging and challenging process for me and I wish everyone there well as they experiment with new ways of what it means to be an Evangelical church in our contemporary world. Ollie Leggett, John Taylor and Derek Willis all read through drafts of various parts of the book and I am very grateful to all of them for their constructive criticism. Any unclear assertions, unsupported arguments or down-right bad jokes that remain in the text are therefore unfortunately my responsibility alone. Finally, as ever, my heartfelt thanks go as well to my family and friends for being with me through all of this.

GORDON LYNCH
March 2003

1
Losing It?

With a book like this, you're really meant to start with a story. A story is a good way of introducing your theme, drawing the reader in, etc., etc. But I've sat for months racking my brains for a suitable story and really have drawn a blank on this. Funnily enough, this isn't because I can't think of any stories at all but because there are so many that I could choose from and I don't know which to choose. I know so many people who grew up with me through Evangelical churches, who went to Christian Union meetings with me, or who I sat with in Bible study groups, who now have either no connection with Evangelical faith at all or who have a quite different relationship to Evangelical beliefs than they did before.

Because the thing is there are significant numbers of people in Evangelical churches who are starting to question their faith or to move from the Evangelical beliefs that they may have lived with for many years. That may seem a surprising suggestion if you are currently in an Evangelical church in which, in public, everyone seems very satisfied with the status quo and no one else seems to be having significant doubts or struggles with their faith. It may also seem a threatening idea as well because for many of us who have been Evangelical Christians, the thought of moving away from Evangelical faith can feel pretty much like moving away from the source of all truth too.

This book is aimed at people who are going precisely through that kind of experience, though. If you've picked this book up, it may be because you're starting to have serious doubts or questions about certain Evangelical beliefs or assumptions. Or it may be because you have been feeling depressed or somehow dissatisfied with your continuing involvement in an Evangelical church. Maybe you know someone who is going through this kind of process of spiritual change and you want to try to understand more about what's happening for them. Or perhaps you don't have a background in Evangelical Christianity at all, but there's something about the book's theme of going through times of spiritual transition and change that interests you.

Whatever brings you to this book, I hope you get something useful from what follows. My aim here is to try to offer an explanation of what the process of moving on from Evangelical faith can be like. In the following pages we'll think about what often causes people to begin to question their Evangelical beliefs, how we can understand the feelings of doubt and confusion that can often be associated with this process, what some of the important losses are that we might face through this time of spiritual change and what resources might help us through it all.

To understand more about these processes we need to begin by thinking about what some of the strengths and weaknesses are of Evangelical Christianity. This will give us a basis for looking, in the next chapter, at what it is that often provokes people to start questioning their Evangelical roots.

So, let's start with the positives.

Four good things about Evangelicalism

Evangelical Christianity, it's not all bad, you know.

Now to get to the point where I could write that first sentence has taken me quite a while. Well, you know, I could have *written* it, but to have written it *and* meant it . . .

For me, though, part of the process of detaching myself from Evangelical Christianity has been to get to the point where I can see positives within it as well as the negatives. This would not always have been the case. Whilst still on the edges of Evangelical churches, I spent a good deal of my time complaining about Evangelicalism. In fact, if there had been some way of converting my moans into electricity, I could probably have single-handedly kept most of my street in heating and lighting without us having to have troubled the electricity board. Rather like being in a relationship or a job that you know isn't good for you but which you haven't been able to get out of, being involved in an Evangelical church when you're not sure that you believe in much of what's going on there, is a hard, depressing and stressful experience. And complaining, either in your own head or to a few select friends, is one way of giving vent to that even if it doesn't necessarily change much in the end.

So for me to say that Evangelical Christianity isn't all bad is genuinely a step forward, I think. But for some people reading this book, it may be a statement that you're not able to make. It may be that you still feel so frustrated, hurt or bruised by your experience of the Church, that the thought of saying this makes you want to weep, hit the nearest cushion or turn the CD player up very loud. In that case, you might want to skip this part of the chapter.

I think it is important to identify positives within Evangelicalism at this point, though. Partly this is because, as the book goes on, I will be saying some fairly clear things about why I think Evangelicalism doesn't always work in spiritually or emotionally healthy ways. I want to start off with some positives as a way of avoiding getting into some kind of theological game of cowboys and indians where Evangelicals are bad and miscellaneous other liberals, radicals, post-Evangelicals and such are good. Churches, like our own selves, are complex mixtures of the good, bad and indifferent, and drawing up caricatures of any one group is not going to help us think more critically and honestly about their strengths and deficiencies.

So here, then, is my list of what I think is good about Evangelicalism (this is, I have to add, a bit different to what John Stott's or Nicky Gumbel's list would look like but there you go):

1. *Evangelicals can have a strong commitment to the principle of helping others and making a positive difference in the world.* I used to work in the world of counselling, as both a counsellor and a counsellor trainer. One of the things that I noticed was that a disproportionately large number of my colleagues and students had some kind of Christian faith (with Evangelicals being well represented amongst them). Some people took a cynical view of this Christian involvement, particularly towards Evangelicals, and suspected that counselling was

being exploited by some Christians as a way of inflicting the gospel message on vulnerable and unsuspecting clients. In general, though, I didn't find that to be the case. People with a Christian faith seemed to be drawn to counselling precisely because something in their faith inclined them to try to help others and this was an honest effort on their part to express that concern.

When I look at the larger picture of Evangelical churches, this kind of concern for others seems to be replicated through a range of activities both in their local communities and internationally. People run lunch clubs out of their churches for elderly people in their local area. Some churches have set up groups to work with asylum seekers. Youth groups have fundraising activities to send money and equipment to orphanages in Romania. Churches support doctors who work in hospitals in developing countries and, thanks to groups such as Tear Fund, the Jubilee 2000 campaign and Christian Aid, are now campaigning on issues of debt and fair trade that are bound up with why the developing world remains poor. If Jesus were to return tomorrow and take his saints to be with him in the sky then (apart from the widespread surprise and consternation this would obviously cause) a significant gap would appear in voluntary work that is done to try to improve people's lives. Obviously important voluntary and social work is done by other non-Evangelical Christian groups, by other faith groups (Buddhist, Hindu, Jewish, Muslim, Sikh, etc.), and by groups with no Church or faith basis at all. But if we were looking around for things to promote a proper sense of 'Evangelical pride', then social concern is one that we could put a tick next to.

2. *Evangelical churches can be communities that welcome in people who might otherwise be socially isolated or displaced.* One day someone will write a good book about loneliness in contemporary society because it is surely one of the big stories about our culture that remains untold. I guess it's not the cheeriest book project for a writer to get their teeth into, though, nor potentially that fun a read either (maybe best to stick with the Harry Potter, after all). But one of the products of a society in which relationships break up with increasing frequency and

where there is rarely much sense of local community, is a greater number of people living what one sociologist has depressingly referred to as 'lonely and prospectless lives'. When we do come together in the main public areas in our towns and cities it is usually to engage in relatively isolated activities such as shopping or going to the cinema. Can you remember the anxiety you probably felt the last time a stranger walked up to you and actually talked to you in a public space? (Readers in London may find this exercise too weird to think about – imagine someone talking to you on the Tube!!) Some of the biggest growth areas in our society in recent years are the online dating agencies and other clubs which offer social or romantic relationships to people who feel lonely or cut off. This sense of loneliness can be further compounded for people with mental health problems. Or for people with learning disabilities. Or for anyone who doesn't always find it easy to mix with other people.

Here's another potential tick in the box for Evangelical pride, then. I have known Evangelical churches to be important social networks for people who might otherwise find their lives much lonelier were it not for this church involvement. Both through formal church activities and through informal social relationships, churches offer a kind of community that isn't always easily accessible elsewhere, unless you're good at salsa dancing or a committed member of your local techno/hard-house club night. If loneliness is one of the most painful afflictions of contemporary society, friendship is the balm that softens the pain of this. Evangelical churches offer people a structure in which they can, at least in principle, be accepted and begin to find friendship.

3. *Evangelicals are often prepared to think and act in counter-cultural ways.* A few years ago, a friend of mine wrote a song called 'We're all going to IKEA', an ironic celebration of the communal joys of shopping for pine shelving and cheap kitchen equipment. Now I really don't have any problems with IKEA in principle (and in fact would currently now be sitting on the floor typing were it not for my IKEA beech-effect dining chair) but there really can be something soul-sapping about a weekend jaunt to the blue and yellow temple.

In fact, a Sunday afternoon trip a while ago to the North London IKEA was the closest I've been to a near-death experience for quite a few years. There's something about the process of following the crowd round the sofas, desks, bedrooms, kitchens, then down, down into the lair of cheap spoons and pot plants, that is a living metaphor for contemporary culture. It feels like we're all walking in the same direction (carefully marshalled by the floor layout of those cunning store designers), buying the same things, blindly sharing the same taste and values, until we finally make it through the tills to the other side and emerge like beached salmon, flapping around and struggling for breath as we reach the open space of the car park. So basically we're born, we shop (in usually not particularly imaginative ways), we die.

Another tick on the growing list of items for Evangelical pride is that Evangelicals are often prepared to ask questions about what life is about and to live in ways that don't necessarily fit with everyday social conventions. When you're growing up as an Evangelical teenager this can feel like, at best, a mixed blessing, but I think a certain amount of credit needs to be given to anyone in today's world who's prepared to think outside of the normal limits.

4. *Evangelicalism has an underlying ethos which can express itself in empowering and democratic ways.* I know someone who has recently completed a major study of the Deaf Church in Britain. One of her main, and very important findings, is that until recently it was assumed that the provision of church services for deaf people was the initiative of hearing clergy in the nineteenth century who took pity on these poor excluded souls and set up church missions to them as an act of charity. In actual fact, deaf congregations were far more often set up by deaf evangelists who were both committed to spreading the gospel amongst the deaf community and to working to improve the social conditions of deaf people. The Evangelical faith of these early deaf missioners was therefore profoundly important in the creation of deaf churches that were not simply appendages to the hearing Church, but places in which the leadership and contribution of deaf members was highly valued.

Now, I don't think it was an accident that these deaf pioneers were Evangelicals. Ideas such as the priesthood of all believers and our personal responsibility for a life of discipleship, evangelism and mission can be genuinely empowering and lead people to live in imaginative ways that benefit both themselves and others. If all believers are priests, heirs in Christ, or whatever your preferred theological concept is, then all members of the Church can find themselves encouraged to discover what mission and ministry means in their own individual situation.

So there we go, four things that I believe are good and important about Evangelicalism. It's important to say that none of these qualities are obviously the sole possession of Evangelical Christianity – plenty of other religious and non-religious individuals and groups demonstrate social concern, a sense of community, counter-cultural thinking and empowerment as well. But these are very important qualities for where we are as a culture in the West today – in fact, I see them as amongst the most important qualities that any group can have right now.

It's also well worth saying that each of these qualities within Evangelicalism has a shadow-side as well. The social concern of Evangelical churches can find expression in practical acts of caring and political campaigning that challenges the injustices currently experienced by the developing world. But in recent years it has also found expression in some churches' support for right-wing social policies that do little to promote human dignity and freedom or to recognise social diversity. Similarly, whilst Evangelical churches have the potential to be supportive, inclusive communities this inclusion can turn out to be dependent on a range of unspoken conditions. People from the wrong ethnic or class background, for example, may find that white, middle-class Evangelical churches are not quite so deeply welcoming as they may at first appear (but, then, few communities are really as inclusive as they look at first sight). The Evangelical readiness to be counter-cultural is potentially a great asset but as many can testify, this can sadly find expression at times in a penchant for strong moral stances on relatively trivial issues and an unfortunate enthusiasm for wearing Oxford-collar shirts underneath woollen jumpers. Ladies and gentlemen of the jury, I present to you Ned Flanders of *The Simpsons*. I rest my case. And the Evangelical ethos of empowerment can find itself sadly undermined by another ethos of control and obedience – more on which shortly.

Again, there is nothing special in Evangelical churches possessing these shadows. All groups and individuals have them and being able to think openly and honestly about these limitations is a first step towards the long and complex process of addressing them. What I have listed here as virtues of Evangelicalism are, I believe, important virtues for our time and long may people continue to live them out.

God loves me! And the catch is . . .?

Here's a bit of a song that I picked out from the latest Spring Harvest song book:

> Light of the World
> you stepped down into darkness
> opened my eyes, let me see.
> Beauty that made this heart adore you,
> hope of a life spent with you.
>
> So here I am to worship,
> here I am to bow down,
> here I am to say that you're my God.
> You're altogether lovely,
> altogether worthy,
> altogether wonderful to me.
>> (Extract taken from the song 'Light of the World' by Tim
>> Hughes. Copyright © 2000 Thankyou Music. Quoted in
>> *Spring Harvest Praise*, Spring Harvest, 2002, p. 26)

Now this seems pretty innocuous and uncontroversial from a Christian perspective. The idea that God loves us and that this love invites a positive response from us is hardly new. Seems to have been a strong theme in Jesus' ministry. Pretty much tied up there with God establishing the covenant with Moses on Mt Sinai

as well, and I guess we could see it going back to the very act of creation itself. Very much an idea with a history behind it, then. So, what's the problem?

At this point I want to introduce an academic idea, though hopefully with a minimum of pain and fuss. This is the idea of *discourse*. Now, recent theories of discourse (you may not be too surprised to discover) have been concerned with exploring how we make sense of the world through the way in which we talk about it. In particular, it has been suggested that we understand the world by making use of particular sets of words and concepts, or 'discourses', that are available to us at our particular time and place in human history. These discourses offer us distinctive concepts or ways of talking about the world that end up being tied up with the way we organise our relationships and the way we relate to each other.

Let me give you an example. My day-to-day work as a lecturer is bound up with an *educational discourse* that provides me and my students with a range of concepts and expectations about how we will relate to each other. To refer to myself as a 'tutor', then, means that we immediately have expectations about what I do in that role (e.g. lead seminars, write course handouts, have tutorials, etc.). Also, and very importantly, it establishes certain power relationships between me as 'tutor' and those people who are 'students' – so, it's me that organises our lessons and determines what we'll do in them and it's me who marks essays and who has the power to pass or fail them. Another thing to notice, as soon as I refer to myself as a 'tutor', is that there are certain things that I would not be expected to do. As a rule, 'tutors' do not generally go round seminar rooms tickling people, nor giving people haircuts. So just by attaching the word 'tutor' to myself and 'student' to the people that I teach, a whole set of expectations, boundaries and power relations get set up between us. A final point on this is that this educational discourse makes sense in a particular context or institutional setting – in my case, a university. Going down to my local branch of Kwik-Save and declaring to the person on the till that I am their tutor and they are my student will seem pretty weird and out of place (though given what my local branch of Kwik-Save is like it probably wouldn't raise too many eyebrows). Similarly going into work tomorrow and telling my students that I am no longer their tutor but a magician will attract attention from the senior management that would be unlikely to help my career development.

So let me quickly re-cap. A 'discourse' is a system of words and concepts that we use to make sense of the world. There are different systems of discourse available to us in the world, though they will only tend to work and make sense if we use them in the right time and place. Discourses aren't simply 'concepts' in an abstract, floaty sense but are ways of talking about the world that have very practical consequences for the expectations that we have of each other and for the powers that we have over people or that they have over us.

So far, so good. Now what I want to suggest is that there is a particular kind of discourse that operates in Evangelical churches. If we were to represent in a kind of diagram the way that this 'Evangelical discourse' makes sense of the world, I think it would look something like this:

GOD/JESUS

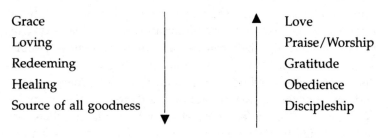

Grace		Love
Loving		Praise/Worship
Redeeming		Gratitude
Healing		Obedience
Source of all goodness		Discipleship

ME

So what we have here is a way of talking about the world that begins with God, or Jesus, and the way that God has acted towards me. God, the source of all goodness, loves me and through an undeserved act of grace He has chosen (through Christ's death) to save and redeem me from sin, death and hell. An appropriate response from me is one of love to God, in which I seek to lead an obedient life of service and discipleship that expresses my gratitude for the good things that God has done for me.

Sound familiar? I suspect that this is the mainstream way of talking about and making sense of the world underlying all that goes on in most Evangelical churches. It finds expression in the words of the worship songs that are sung, in the prayers that are made, in the ultimate message of the sermons that are preached and in the lessons that are taken from studying the Bible. Charismatic Evangelical churches have a whole other layer of discourse that relates to how the Holy Spirit and spiritual gifts are talked about but I think that this Charismatic layer is added to, rather than fundamentally changing, this basic pattern of Evangelical discourse.

Now, at this point, we could get into a theological debate about whether this particular way of talking about the world is a good and full reflection of the Christian scriptures and tradition. I think there are other people who can do a better job of discussing that than me, and anyway I want to look at this 'Evangelical discourse' not so much from a theological point of view, but from a practical point of view. Basically, what I want to do now is to think about what kind of effects this way of talking about the world has on ourselves and our relationships with others.

From my point of view, I can see certain benefits and certain problems with this particular system of concepts.

The benefits

- Having God as the starting point of this system is a really important reminder that our individual lives are a *gift* to us and not something we have created ourselves. In an age of self-made men and women this can hopefully teach us some humility, respect and awe at the mysteries of the greater reality in which we have been given the chance to take part.
- The message that God, who stands at the very heart of existence, loves us, is clearly a profoundly positive one. The belief that we are deeply loved by the creator of the universe can inspire lives that are courageous and hopeful.
- This system provides a clear structure within which we can focus our emotional and spiritual energy. Without deriding it by saying this, there is an obvious simplicity to this idea of our spiritual lives as an act of receiving and reciprocating

God's love for us. It is this simplicity that can enable diverse groups of people to come together around this central spiritual message and which can provide many people with a strong sense of religious direction in their lives.

From these positive points it is easy to see how an Evangelical system of discourse can have a strong appeal and have beneficial effects in many people's lives.

In terms of the way that this Evangelical system of discourse operates in the real world, though, I'd suggest that there are some serious down-sides as well.

The down-sides

- It is a very 'top-down' way of thinking about life. God is above me and I am a sinner, utterly dependent on God's love and grace. A fair theological point, you might say, but if we think about this in terms of power relations then God is powerful and I am largely powerless. This becomes particularly problematic in the day-to-day lives of churches when ministers or church leaders become wittingly or unwittingly associated with God and these same power inequalities get played out between them and their congregations. This way of thinking can therefore reinforce hierarchical church structures in which those who represent God's truth get to tell others what to do and how to live their lives. A related problem here is the issue of gender. Evangelical discourse almost always refers to God as a male figure and so we find that it tends to generate not only hierarchical church structures, but *patriarchal* structures too, in which it becomes an assumed fact of life that men hold the majority of the power. How many Evangelical churches do you know whose overall leader is a woman?
- If God is above me and the source of all goodness and truth, then it follows that I can only really learn about myself or about how I should live my life by learning 'top-down' from God – or, more usually, from the mediators of God's message, i.e. preachers, Bible study notes, books and tapes from sound and approved Evangelicals. The possibility that I might be able to learn more about myself, God or life in general through

exploring the meaning of my own experience therefore tends to get forgotten. Similarly the possibility that I might be able to learn something profound from people who are not Evangelicals, or not even (God forbid) Christians, tends to get excluded too. We'll come back to this point in more detail in the next chapter.

• The idea of a life lived in response to God's love may not be that controversial in the context of Christian beliefs but where things get more tricky is in the precise nature of obedient Christian discipleship. What if the standards of Christian living set down by Evangelical discourse turned out to be somewhat arbitrary? Or even downright wrong in places? The difficult thing here is raising serious questions about these things because to do so can immediately appear to challenge the truth that has come down to us from God and therefore constitutes a fundamental act of ingratitude and disobedience on our part. So this way of talking in terms of a life of obedient discipleship can become something of a straight-jacket on our ability to think openly about how we should live our lives.

Here's the rub, then. God loves us and this is obviously a good thing. But the way in which this love is understood in Evangelical discourse tends to support hierarchical and patriarchal structures, a dependence on 'approved' Evangelical sources for finding out the truth about life, and a pressure to conform to certain standards of behaviour whether or not these are really essential to a morally and spiritually healthy life.

If we can live with the benefits of Evangelicalism and not feel too bothered or maybe not even notice these down-sides, then this Evangelical discourse can indeed be an on-going source of strength and hope in our lives. When we start to notice the down-sides, though, and start realising how serious they are, then we're into a whole new, long hard journey. In the next chapter, we'll see how this journey often starts.

2
On the Dangers of Experience

I found it became impossible to propound an official point of view like a political speaker taking a party line. Such a procedure appeared so false to myself that the words would not come. Unless what I proposed to say came from the depths of my own experience, I was struck dumb ... All I could speak of were those things which I had proved true in my own experience by living them and thus knowing them at first hand.

(Harry Williams, *The True Wilderness*, Constable, 1965, pp. 8–9)

I have a theory about what leads people to start asking deep and searching questions about their Evangelical faith or the Evangelical churches of which they have been members.

I think that for many people, Evangelical faith is like Holland. No, I don't mean that it's characterised by tulips, good football and a liberal drugs policy. What I had in mind is that Evangelical faith is often like land that has been reclaimed from the sea, with the sea being held back by a strong, water-tight wall. This arrangement can work pretty well as long as the wall stays water-tight, but if a small crack or leak appears in the wall this can start to let a steady drip of water through. Over time the leak gets a bit bigger and the wall starts to weaken. Another leak appears. Then another. Until a number of streams of water start pouring through and the staple crop for farmers stops being tulips and becomes rice instead.

Evangelical faith can be like this scenario. In the last chapter, we hinted at the idea that Evangelical discourse can make a very clear and rigid separation between things that are good and bad. This sometimes works along the following lines:

Things that are good (according to Evangelical discourse)

1. the Bible;
2. prayer meetings;
3. singing worship songs (and meaning them at the same time);
4. sermons that provide good, biblical truths;
5. marriage;
6. families;
7. good, informal, clean fun;
8. bring and share meals;
9. Bible study groups;
10. sensible clothing (e.g. jumpers worn over Oxford-collar shirts, sorry did I mention that already . . .?).

And then,

Things that are bad (according to Evangelical discourse)

1. sex outside marriage;
2. definitely gay sex, if you didn't realise that was covered by the previous point;
3. dressing in a way that makes other people think about sex;
4. looking too much at other people who are dressed in a way that makes you think about sex;
5. smoking (tobacco that is, cannabis tends not to register on the radar here);
6. drinking to the point of slurred speech and prolonged, inexplicable laughter;
7. swearing (though things are softening and you might be able to get away with a b-word and a d-word, though s- and f-words are still not advised);
8. cohabitation (sharing the gas and electricity bills isn't the problem here, but it's the sex with someone you're not married to that's the issue – so we're back to the first point);
9. saying that you have basic questions/problems with a) the

Bible, b) prayer meetings, c) sermons delivering biblical truths, d) Bible study groups, e) bring and share lunches, f) marriage, g) families (or church family services in particular), h) good, clean, informal fun, i) the Alpha course, j) spending your leisure time at Spring Harvest or some other prayer and worship-fest, or k) any combination of the above;

10. writing tongue-in-cheek compilations about things that are good and bad according to Evangelicalism (especially if they go on too much about sex).

Well, that was fun. On a quiet evening in, you might want to make up your own top ten list of good and bad things too. Now where was I?

Oh, yes. Now Evangelicalism has tended to make quite clear markers between ideas, beliefs and lifestyles which it sees as acceptable and those which it sees as unacceptable. These clear lines of demarcation can work well just so long as a) you have a group of people around you who reinforce these beliefs about what is acceptable and what is not, and b) you don't encounter anyone, or have an experience, that fundamentally challenges them.

So to get, eventually, to the point, my theory is that people start raising questions about their Evangelical beliefs, and their particular Evangelical church, when they have some kind of encounter with someone or some kind of experience that challenges their previous Evangelical assumptions. Because Evangelical boundaries between what is right and wrong have traditionally been quite rigid, one experience that raises questions and doubts tends to generate other questions and doubts that can lead over time to a more wholesale questioning of the Evangelical way of looking at life.

These experiences, which are the equivalent of poking a hole in the metaphorical dyke that we mentioned earlier, might take two different broad types. You'll remember that in the last chapter I pushed the boundaries of my graphic design skills to bring you a diagrammatic representation of what I saw as the structure of mainstream Evangelical discourse. One important aspect of this is God's gracious acts of love in redeeming and healing us. The other is our grateful response to God's goodness, which takes the form of a life of obedience and discipleship. Now the two different types of experience that can fundamentally challenge Evangelical faith are precisely those that raise questions either about God's loving goodness to us or about the true nature of the Christian lifestyle.

For example, I remember many years ago talking to one of the people who was helping to lead a Christian Union weekend that I was attending. Chatting to him, at one point, he began to talk about a recent experience of his son being seriously ill. As a committed Evangelical, this man had prayed to God to relieve his son's suffering and to bring him healing. But nothing had happened. On the basis of this experience, the father began to question whether God's goodness was always as immediately evident in the world as Evangelical discourse seems to suggest and over time he turned to a different style of prayer that was completely different to the intercessory style he had grown up with. Some people might look at this person and say, 'If only he'd had more faith to persist in his prayers to God for healing!' But I think anyone who knows something of the heartbreak this man felt at the persistence of his son's illness and the absence of any divine healing or comfort in the midst of it, would be more cautious in their response.

Funnily enough, this kind of heart-rending experience is not unknown in the pages of the Bible either. The book of Lamentations, for example, contains a lot of harsh words about a God who has given up on the covenant He made with the people of Israel and has abandoned His city of Jerusalem to the point where its inhabitants are reduced to eating the dead bodies of children in order to survive.

Now, there have unquestionably been times when some Evangelical responses to people's experiences of suffering have been shallow and trite. At the same time, it's important to recognise others within Evangelical churches who experience suffering of a kind that I'm grateful not to have experienced, yet who retain a clear and committed Evangelical faith. The depth of their spirituality should give pause for thought for jaded old cynics like me. But equally, it's important to recognise that for others in Evangelical churches, the experience of suffering can lead them to raise fundamental questions about Evangelical stock-phrases about God's goodness to us. Such an experience can therefore be one kind of catalyst that leads to deeper, more fundamental questions about the received truths of Evangelicalism. Related kinds of experience are those in which someone comes to realise that a particular church leader, who has previously been seen as a mediator of God's goodness, might not be quite such a benevolent figure as was first imagined.

The other kind of experience that I have in mind is one that challenges our ideas about what it really means to live a good, Christian life. Some years ago, I developed a friendship with someone in a Christian organisation whose spirituality deeply impressed me. Let's call him Gareth, for the sake of argument and anonymity. I would say, without intending to embarrass him, that Gareth has a greater depth to his spiritual life than most people I have met. I saw early on that he was a skilled communicator and a sensitive and able pastor, and I am not surprised that the Christian groups that Gareth has worked with have highly valued the time he has spent with them. What was a surprise for me, and for him as well really, was his growing recognition that he was gay. Given the Evangelical background he'd come from, this was obviously a difficult part of himself to acknowledge. But as he recognised his sexual orientation and began to explore a wide range of Christian thinking about gay sexuality, he came to the honest conviction that he could be in a gay relationship and retain the integrity of his Christian faith.

As it happens, he has been in a gay relationship for some time now. And also, as it happens, that relationship has lasted longer than the marriages of several of us who were in that particular group of friends. And again, as it happens, not many of the people that he worked with in Christian settings knew that he was gay. And I guess that if they'd found out, then that simple fact would have made a real difference to how some of them would have perceived him – a person who they'd otherwise seen as one of the most able people to have worked with them.

Now before I knew Gareth, I used to have a John Stott-like view on issues of gay sexuality. Which means that I believed that, whilst God deeply loved gay men and lesbians, He also had condemned gay sexual acts and so a life of celibacy was the only valid Christian option for them. I was already starting to wonder about that before Gareth came out as gay but seeing his experience really put the nails in the coffin of my Evangelical beliefs on this issue. One of the parts of Jesus' teaching that I take particularly seriously is his idea that you will know about the nature of a person's character by the fruits of their lives. The 'fruit' of Gareth's life suggests to me that the path he is pursuing is a spiritually and morally healthy one. Yet, this evidence would be rejected by some people in the Church purely on the basis of his sexual orientation. And the fact that I cannot tell you here the real name of someone whose work and lifestyle I feel so positively about is an indication that we are not living in times that are showing many signs of becoming more liberal or tolerant.

My friendship with Gareth therefore raised fundamental questions for me about the validity of gay relationships within a committed Christian lifestyle. And I ended up coming down on the side of answers that remain unacceptable within the definitions of what is good and bad in Evangelical discourse. And as with the metaphor of the dyke, this leak in my Evangelical orthodoxy began to connect up to other questions, other leaks, until the whole structure of my Evangelical faith was wobbling like a Jenga tower in its last death throes.

So, that's my theory of why many people start to question seriously their Evangelical beliefs and affiliation. It's experiences that can't be fitted neatly into Evangelical discourse that do it, not lack of faith, or the devil, or some kind of lax, corrosive theological liberalism. It is real, heartfelt experiences of pain, friendship and love that open up the door to new ways of looking at the world.

Listening to our experiences

If my theory about why people start to question their Evangelical beliefs is correct, then we can see how a wide range of different experiences can set people off on this journey. Seeds of doubt about the received truths of Evangelicalism can therefore be sown by any or all of the following:

- learning something important or profound from a person or source that is not generally 'approved of' in Evangelical circles;
- friendships with people who are not Evangelical Christians, which lead to a respect for the integrity of their non-Evangelical lifestyles;
- a realisation that a particular behaviour condemned in Evangelical circles may not be as damaging as it is portrayed (in fact, it might even be helpful or healing);
- experiences that lead to the realisation that Evangelical churches are not perfect loving communities but that they are as flawed as any other human institution or group;
- experiences of suffering that challenge simplistic ideas about how God will make things better for those who have enough faith, or which raise even more basic questions about how God is present to us at all;
- a growing sense of boredom with Evangelical church activities that leads to the realisation that they are not as emotionally, relationally or spiritually stimulating as we once found them to be;
- a sense of excitement, energy or freedom in spending time in non-church activities;
- recognising that our life experience, our values, or our interests and concerns don't really fit into the mould of the standard Evangelical lifestyle.

Anyone who has stepped out on to the road of questioning their Evangelical roots will have their own story about what set them off, which might include any of the above experiences or many more. For those of us who have started out on that route, learning to tell the story of how we came to begin to question Evangelicalism, or move away from it, is an important thing to do. We'll come back to this point in chapter five.

A basic doubt, though, for anyone reared in Evangelicalism who is starting to question things in this way can be whether it is right to give such weight to our personal experiences. Should our lives, after all, not be based on the timeless Word of God, rather than the shifting, emotionally complex sands of our own lives?

I'm sure some years ago I would have said that the Word of

God was where it was all at. Now, I would say that any attempt to live a life based on a fundamental denial or distortion of our own experience of ourselves, other people or God invites disaster for our own mental and spiritual well-being and for our relationships with those around us.

One of the things that set me off on changing my mind on this issue was getting involved in the world of counselling. When I first started to get interested in what counsellors did and how they thought about their work, someone suggested that I should read some of the work of Carl Rogers. I'd never heard of him before but it turned out that he was an American psychologist whose work had a major impact on the counselling scene across the world. I picked up his book *On Becoming a Person* and found that the first chapter was one in which he was talking about the main lessons he had learnt from over thirty years of working as a psychologist and therapist. Expecting to find some rather dry, psychological discussion about mental health, I was astonished at what I read:

I would like to take you inside, to tell you some of the things I have learned from the thousands of hours I have spent working intimately with individuals in personal distress. I would like to make it very plain that these are learnings which have significance for *me*. I do not know whether they would hold true for you. I have no desire to present them as a guide for anyone else. Yet I have found that when another person has been willing to tell me something of his (sic) inner directions this has been of value to me, if only in sharpening my realization that my directions are different . . . They are certainly scattered learnings and incomplete. I can only say that they are and have been very important to me. I continually learn and re-learn them. I frequently fail to act in terms of them, but later wish that I had . . .

I might start off these several statements of significant learnings with a negative item. *In my relationships with persons I have found that it does not help, in the long run, to act as though I were something that I am not* . . . A second learning might be stated as follows – *I find I am more effective when I can listen acceptantly to myself, and can be myself . . .* [Further-more] *I have found it enriching to open channels whereby others communicate their feelings, their private perceptual words to me . . . I have found it highly rewarding to accept another person . . . The more I am open to the realities in me and in the other person, the less do I find myself wishing to rush in and 'fix things' . . . I can trust my experience . . . Experience is, for me, the highest authority.*

(Carl Rogers, *On Becoming a Person*, Constable, 1961,
pp. 15–23)

My reaction at reading these words was a strange mix of horror, delight and discomfort. Firstly I was thrown by his disarming lack of interest in imposing his views on others and his acknow-ledgement that others might take quite different lessons from life to those that he had done. Then I was thrown even more by his simple and honest stance of self-acceptance (shouldn't he feel more aware of his innate sinfulness?). This was someone whose work had a huge international impact, who in his own way became as significant for modern therapy as more famous names like Sigmund Freud and Carl Jung. Yet his learning about therapy could be distilled into these simple statements about the import-ance of accepting and listening to both our own experience and the experience of other people. I felt that somehow he was saying something terribly important about life and yet also that he was saying something that I found very threatening.

It may or may not come as a surprise to you that Carl Rogers' own journey to this set of beliefs about life began from his background in the Evangelical Church. In fact, as a young man Rogers was an enthusiastic Christian and was seen as a potential Evangelical leader. Quite how he got from there to being a leading humanistic psychologist is a long story for another day.

When Rogers reminisced about his childhood, growing up in an Evangelical household, there were two religious phrases that really stayed with him as summing up his family's beliefs: 'All our righteousness is as filthy rags in thy sight, O Lord' and 'Come out from among them and be ye separate'. The first phrase emphasised how unutterably sinful we all were and the second indicated that despite this, those outside the Church were even more unutterably sinful and a dreadful source of temptation to stray from the path of righteousness. The beliefs that Rogers grew up with at the start of his life and those he had developed by the end of his professional career were therefore poles apart, with ideas of sin, guilt and obedience to God being replaced by acceptance of self and others and a valuing of whatever our experience has to teach us.

Now, I'm not suggesting that Carl Rogers' life and thought represent the answers to all our questions – in fact, a recent hatchet job of a biography of his life certainly makes it harder to turn him into some kind of secular saint. Rather like the rest of us, it turns out that Rogers was a flawed person with his own weaknesses and struggles. But I do think that the beliefs of Rogers' early life and those of his later life represent two strongly contrasting positions between which people who are questioning their Evangelical roots have to negotiate their way. On the one hand, there is his early strong faith in the truth of the Word of God as the basis for life. And on the other, there is his later belief in the importance of accepting ourselves and other people as we are, and being prepared, above all things, to learn whatever lessons our experience has to teach us.

Now, there are reasonable psychological grounds to suggest that if an emphasis on believing some kind of external truth, such as 'biblical teaching', leads us to deny or repress what is going on in our inner spiritual and emotional life this will bear a range of fruits such as loneliness, depression, anxiety and panic attacks. Similarly a lack of healthy contact with our own emotional life can lead, for some people, to eating disorders or self-harm. Being open to what we are really experiencing is vital for our emotional and spiritual survival as human beings. But if we value our experience more than the Word of God when there seems to be a conflict between the two, are we not being profoundly disloyal or disobedient to the spiritual life that we should be living?

Well, in a word, I would say no. Up until now in this chapter I have been using the phrase 'the Word of God' in the sense that it is commonly meant in Evangelical discourse, i.e. as the truth about God and ourselves as revealed to us through the Bible.

Perhaps we could think about God's Word in our lives in a slightly different way.

Ignatius of Loyola was born in 1491 and for much of his early life was a page and a soldier in northern Spain. Following a serious injury sustained in battle, Ignatius was forced to spend time recuperating back at his home in the castle at Loyola. During this period his own spiritual life began to open up for him in new ways and he discovered the importance of paying attention to the movements of his inner life for his on-going relationship with God. He later went on to write about his understanding of the spiritual life in his book *The Spiritual Exercises*. In part of this book, he wrote:

> It is wisely said, 'Experience is the best teacher' ... The primary and most obvious reason for this is that revelation is not over, God is constantly revealing himself to us in our experience ... Of course, the Bible is divine revelation – no one denies that. But so is life! It is precisely because God is present to life and available to human experience that *we* have a divinely inspired story to tell, and that story once told is revelation.
>
> (quoted in D. Linn, S. Fabricant Linn and M. Linn,
> *Sleeping with Bread: Holding What Gives You Life*,
> Paulist Press, 1995, p. 19)

Ignatius of Loyola therefore had a somewhat different idea of God's Word than that of mainstream Evangelicalism. Rather than seeing God's Word as something purely beyond us and above us that comes from outside us in the form of Scripture to enlighten and guide us, Ignatius saw our experience as being a crucial way in which divine truth could be revealed to us. So we can learn more about God's truth in our lives by paying attention to what gives us emotional and spiritual energy (and conversely what leaves us feeling dead or empty). Or we can learn more by exploring what thoughts and feelings come up for us when we pray or imagine ourselves into scenes from the Bible. Or we can learn more by paying attention to what we learn about ourselves from our different life experiences and from listening carefully to others' life experiences too. God's truth, according to Ignatius, does not therefore come neatly packaged in a well-delivered sermon or beautifully published paperback but through listening to our own experiences and learning more about the truth about ourselves and God from that.

You may well have spotted in this quote that Ignatius by no means dismisses the significance of the Bible as a way of God revealing truth to us. And for many people who are questioning their Evangelical beliefs the Bible, or maybe a wider understanding of Christian tradition, will still be important in helping them to make sense of their lives. But what I take from Ignatius' words here is the idea that even if we still turn to the Bible for a sense of direction and meaning in life, our reading of the Bible will be transformed if we bring to it the serious questions and lessons that we have taken from our own experience. To give an example, before I met Gareth I would have read the Bible as condemning gay sexual relationships. Having learnt from my friendship with him, I now believe that if the Bible is a source of truth then it cannot condemn the life that he leads. Taking our own experiences seriously therefore changes the kind of relationship that we have with the pages of Scripture. This relationship begins to turn this more into a conversation rather than a monologue in which one particular interpretation of the Bible is assumed to have the final word over anything that I have learnt from my own life.

Now, I really think that what people like Harry Williams, Carl Rogers and Ignatius of Loyola have to say about the significance of being true to ourselves and to our own experience is really important. It's taken me a long time to really even begin to appreciate it. For ages, I was an avid reader of books on religion and spirituality, keenly hoping that one day I would discover the book that would give me all the answers to my spiritual searching. Over time, though, I've come to realise that whilst listening to the wisdom of other writers can be very helpful, my spiritual life can ultimately only be grounded in what I find to be meaningful and true in my own experience.

To the ears of mainstream Evangelical discourse that can sound incredibly arrogant. Am I not placing myself above God's truth as revealed in the Bible? And besides, how trustworthy really is our experience? Can't we be wrong about our feelings or spiritual experience? Am I just advocating a 'do what feels good to you' spirituality?

Well, yes, there are problems with the idea of basing our spiritual lives on the truths that we learn from our experience. Acting purely on the basis of our immediate feelings can be the right thing to do in some instances. But as a general lifestyle, simply acting out our immediate feelings tends to produce chaotic lives and fragmented relationships. We can sometimes have very partial, and indeed self-deceiving, understandings of our experiences that tend to make it harder for us to detect our prejudices, intellectual laziness or vested self-interest. We can also be absorbed in our own lives to a degree that becomes unhealthy if we are chronically unable to take account of others' views or experiences. All of this is possible, which is why it is important to have good friendships in which people are able to be honest with us and put our experiences and perceptions into some wider context. And which is why it is important to have the kind of humility Carl Rogers talked about, in being prepared to continually revise and renew what we learn about ourselves and other people.

But despite these difficulties, I would still claim that being true to our experience is the best route to an intellectually, emotionally and spiritually healthy life. It turns out, anyway, that these same problems beset those who seek to base their lives primarily on the truth of the Bible. Uncritical and unthinking use of Scripture can turn out to be as damaging a foundation for life as an unthinking approach towards our emotions. And interpretations of Scripture can be equally prey to self-deception and vested interest as any interpretations of our own experiences.

But in the end all of this can turn into a lot of theological hot air. If you have been driven to start questioning your Evangelical beliefs or your church's teaching because of particular experiences that you've had, then abstract theological debates about how we discover truth won't put the brakes on this process. The emotional pull of the truth of our experiences is very powerful and when you've had certain experiences it becomes more or less impossible not to start asking wider questions. Once you start to do that, though, it can begin to feel like you're falling through space or sinking into sand. And it's that feeling that we'll look at more in the next chapter.

3
Meeting God in the Car Park of Doubt

Last night I went to see the new *Lord of the Rings* film. I was relieved that Derek (one of the friends that I saw it with) did not come dressed in chain-mail or full-on wizard gear, given that he is more enthusiastic about this kind of thing than the average person. On the way back, though, he did more than once refer to me as Gordon, son of Gloin, bearer of the broken Peugeot 106. I mention this, not because it has any particular relevance to what follows in this chapter, but simply as a warning to keep your children and other loved ones away from playing too much Dungeons and Dragons during their formative years.

I was going to say something about *Lord of the Rings*, though. What may well have struck you from the films – or the brave amongst you who have read what feels like the two million pages of the actual book – is the sheer scale of the journey that the central characters undertake. In fact the book, with its long descriptions of the journey and the landscapes that are being travelled through, conveys this even better than the films. This sense of epic journey is one that is generally quite alien to our contemporary experience. Modern technologies of travel mean that we are increasingly used to travelling large distances in comparatively short spaces of time unless you are travelling on the British rail network or using the M6. In fact, if Frodo Baggins had access to a Lear Jet, he could have nipped over to Mordor and back in time for tea, though this would have made for a rather different film.

The point that I'm meandering towards is that our sense of space and time in the contemporary world has kind of collapsed.

through space or sinking into sand. And it's that feeling that we'll look at more in the next chapter.

3
Meeting God in the Car Park of Doubt

Last night I went to see the new *Lord of the Rings* film. I was relieved that Derek (one of the friends that I saw it with) did not come dressed in chain-mail or full-on wizard gear, given that he is more enthusiastic about this kind of thing than the average person. On the way back, though, he did more than once refer to me as Gordon, son of Gloin, bearer of the broken Peugeot 106. I mention this, not because it has any particular relevance to what follows in this chapter, but simply as a warning to keep your children and other loved ones away from playing too much Dungeons and Dragons during their formative years.

I was going to say something about *Lord of the Rings*, though. What may well have struck you from the films – or the brave amongst you who have read what feels like the two million pages of the actual book – is the sheer scale of the journey that the central characters undertake. In fact the book, with its long descriptions of the journey and the landscapes that are being travelled through, conveys this even better than the films. This sense of epic journey is one that is generally quite alien to our contemporary experience. Modern technologies of travel mean that we are increasingly used to travelling large distances in comparatively short spaces of time unless you are travelling on the British rail network or using the M6. In fact, if Frodo Baggins had access to a Lear Jet, he could have nipped over to Mordor and back in time for tea, though this would have made for a rather different film.

The point that I'm meandering towards is that our sense of space and time in the contemporary world has kind of collapsed.

I can travel from my flat to the other side of the world in just over a day. Though often, if I was travelling just to talk to someone, it would make more sense to pick up the phone or send them an e-mail and I can be in touch with them immediately. This leaves us with a quite different way of thinking about the world to the characters of *Lord of the Rings*. Words like 'season' and 'journey' have less immediate meaning for us in a world in which supermarkets provide much the same vegetables all the year round and in which travelling large distances involves so much less time and hardship than in the days when people travelled by foot, carriage or boat.

One of the important effects of our changed sense of time and space is that it makes us less in touch with our emotional and spiritual lives. Whilst at the level of ideas, desires and expectations about life, we live at the pace of high-speed travel and immediate electronic communication, our emotional and spiritual life proceeds more at the pace of a gentle stroll across Middle Earth. We still have words like 'season' and 'journey' in our vocabulary but have less sense of how long the seasons of grief take to pass or how long a spiritual journey can really take.

And once we have had the kind of experiences or started to ask the kind of questions that we looked at in the previous chapter then we usually have embarked on a long journey towards a new form of faith and self-understanding. One of the strange features of this journey for many people, though, is that they are not aware that they are on a journey at all until they are some way into it. This is the spiritual and emotional equivalent of living in Kent and waking up one day to find yourself on a train half way to Aberdeen and can be just as disconcerting.

In the first chapter, I wrote about going through a long period of being both involved in Evangelical churches and moaning a lot about them at the same time. Now this kind of experience is a good example of how our emotional and spiritual lives may have set off on a journey of which we are not yet consciously aware. Indeed, for me, it was only after a few years of complaining and hanging around the edges of church, that I was able consciously to face how deeply my sense of disconnection with Evangelical Christianity really ran. Others have similar experiences of living for years with a vague sense of boredom, tiredness or dissatisfaction in relation to their church lives, without necessarily seeing this as a symptom of a deeper and gradual spiritual process of separation and change.

I think that there can be a number of reasons why people who are beginning to become emotionally and spiritually disconnected from Evangelical Christianity can find it hard to face up to this or be aware of it. These include:

1. *Feeling that you are letting God down.* We saw in chapter one how Evangelical discourse sets up a certain relationship in which God's love for us requires a loving and obedient response from us in return. In Evangelical discourse, this obedient response involves accepting core Evangelical ideas about God, salvation, prayer and how you should live as a disciple of Christ. Raising basic questions or doubts about any of these ideas can leave us feeling that we are failing to honour our side of the proper relationship with God and that we do not have sufficient faith and love. This is ironic given that, as we saw in the last chapter, the questions and doubts that arise out of our experiences are a fundamental way in which God's truth can be discovered in our lives.

2. *Feeling that you may be letting other people down if you are too open about your questions, experiences and doubts.* The often rigid nature of Evangelical beliefs about God and appropriate Christian lifestyle can be accompanied by a subtle sense that too much questioning can be dangerous and undermine proper faith in God. The implication here can therefore be that faith is a fragile thing that may not stand up to honest intellectual and emotional scrutiny. For some people, then, it can feel like if they are too vocal about their negative perceptions of Evangelicalism this could harm other people's faith in God. Or if not actually damaging others' faith, it can feel like to be honest would provoke feelings of disappointment in others which again is something we will not particularly want to do.

3. *Realising that other people in the church may well not want to hear about your questions and doubts.* Another aspect of the kind of defensiveness alluded to in (2.) is that when people do raise honest questions or talk openly about experiences that don't

fit neatly within Evangelical expectations, they may find that others in the church either don't want to listen or simply struggle to grasp what you are saying. I remember one Bible study group meeting in which I spoke about my growing doubts about traditional Evangelical views of homosexuality. The group's reaction varied from horror to bemusement to a basic struggle to understand that I really did mean what I was saying. Experiences like this can teach us to be much more cautious about saying what we really think about things but can also make it harder for us to reflect openly in our own heads about our changing views and beliefs.

4. *Earning a living from the church in some way (e.g. as a church leader or youth worker)*. Church workers are in no way immune from the kind of doubts and experiences we've been exploring; indeed they may be particularly aware of the flaws in the organisations that they work in. Dwelling too much on your doubts about Evangelicalism can be hard, though, when it's an Evangelical church or organisation that pays your salary.

Now counsellors and therapists, often influenced by Carl Rogers' work, have consistently found that there are certain conditions that a person needs to be able to explore their deeper thoughts, feelings and spiritual life in an open and honest way. One of the key things is that if a person is talking to someone else about their experience and inner life, then they need to feel accepted and understood by that other person. The more a person feels that they can be allowed to say anything, the more open they are likely to be in their reflections about themselves and others. Another key thing is that a person can only really begin this process of self-exploration if they begin to remove forms of self-censorship that stop them from being aware of what they are really thinking or feeling.

When we look again at this list of points we can see how they can contribute to an emotional environment in which it becomes much harder to think honestly about our questions and doubts about Evangelical faith. If I believe that to doubt or question is to let God down in some way, then this will immediately set up mechanisms in which I consciously or unconsciously try to censor or filter out thoughts that I imagine will displease God. If I believe that talking openly about my experience will harm others' faith, or that people will not accept or understand me if I do, then again this will make me very wary of trying to think out loud with other people about my questions, feelings and ideas. These kind of barriers, either within our own minds or within our opportunities for communicating honestly with others, can therefore make it much harder for us to focus openly on the real movements of our emotional and spiritual lives. And a whole other set of difficulties arise as well if the people with whom we now find honest communication hard include our partners or people who have been very close friends.

So, while the pace of our emotional and spiritual journeys may be slow, these journeys can also be hidden from us until the point when something happens to make us realise that we have moved a long way from our Evangelical homes and that things are never going to be quite the same again. And when that happens . . .

Apophatic spirituality and the car park of doubt

In *Pilgrim's Progress*, John Bunyan wrote about the Slough of Despond. Whilst not really being in the same league as John Bunyan as a writer, I would nevertheless like to try and update his language for a more modern, urban readership and talk instead about the car park of doubt and uncertainty.

One thing that I have found from my own experience and from the experiences of others that I've spoken to is that when people become more aware of having started to move away from their Evangelical roots they often feel much clearer about what they *don't* believe than what they *do*. A few years ago, I made the following note in my journal:

> I'm sitting here, as dusk falls this evening, wondering what to write . . . I feel I am experiencing a loss of faith. Part of me feels like drawing a thick black line between all I have written before [in the journal] and this, because it feels like I (or something) has changed irrevocably, that I can't feel in

the same way as I used to, that I can't identify with what I have thought and said about God in the past ... I followed the path that I believed God wanted for me ... Now I have come to the end of the path, and it seems to be the end of any sign-posts as well. My uncertainties about God make it difficult to hope for divine guidance or to expect or experience the sense of direction I have had before ... So here I am, standing on a barren heath, wondering how I got here and where I should go now.

Looking through the previous pages of the journal it looks like this entry really was a flash of new insight. The fact that I hadn't written much in it for the previous six months also suggests I might have been trying not to think too much about my spiritual life up to that point. And I am very much struck by this experience being one of *negation*, of being clear that I no longer believed in a certain kind of God or a certain kind of divine intervention in the world, and this leaving me with a landscape with no sign-posts. We could think about this experience as part of a process of *deconstruction*, of having our previous beliefs pulled down but not yet having any new ones to stand in their place.

This is where, arguably, the metaphor of the car park comes in. The car park is often an integral part of making a journey to somewhere that we want to get to. The car park isn't usually our destination but a means to being able to get to our destination. Hanging about in car parks is not a particularly enjoyable or meaningful thing to do, unless you're some kind of car-spotter. And if we find ourselves spending time in a car park it is usually an experience of waiting – waiting for someone that we're picking up or waiting for a shop or club to open.

If we are at a point where our religious beliefs have fallen away, but not yet been replaced by new understandings of ourselves or God, then this is a very car park-like experience. It is a transition, a point between two places; a place where we need to spend time in order to change and move to something new. But it is also a place that is not necessarily that attractive or enjoyable. The feelings that we might have with this kind of experience could include loneliness, confusion, doubt, depression and anxiety, as well as possibly a sense of freedom or relief at having moved on from something that really just wasn't working out.

In the midst of this doubt and uncertainty, there are certain things that we can still hold on to. One is that, although your experience may currently be one of simply not knowing what you believe in, there will over time be a process of *reconstruction* in which you begin to discover a firmer footing for your spiritual life. Again, the slow pace of this journey is worth bearing in mind. It is a process that will take some years – in fact the journal entry I included earlier was written over seven years ago and much of that time since has been a slow and gradual reconstruction of new forms of belief for me. But given time and the right kind of support, this process will take place. I don't imagine that we ever reach a place of final answers whilst we still have breath in our bodies. But I do believe it is possible to move from a place in which we are most aware of our doubts and uncertainties to a place in which we have more confidence in our beliefs and a greater sense of contentment and peace about our lives.

Another important point to make, though, is that an experience of *negation*, of not knowing what to say or believe about God, actually points us to a significant tradition in Christian theology that is rarely spoken about in Evangelical churches. This is the tradition of *apophatic* theology and spirituality, which is usually associated with particular traditions of Christian mysticism.

The basic assumption of apophatic (or 'negative') theology is that it is not possible to give an adequate representation of what God is like through any words, concepts or symbols. God is above and beyond any language that we can use to describe God, or as one mystical writer put it, God is enclosed in a 'cloud of unknowing' which can only be pierced with darts of love.

One of the leading writers in this mystical tradition was a German theologian, Meister Eckhart, who wrote and preached around the turn of the fourteenth century. Despite being one of the leading theologians of his day, Eckhart was not always one for toeing an orthodox line and spent the last three years of his life under the cloud of an inquisition into his 'heretical' teachings – a fact that might make him appeal even more to people of a post-Evangelical persuasion.

When we look at some of Eckhart's sermons, we can see that he had some extraordinary things to say about the nature of our encounter with God. Here are a couple:

> I have spoken of a power in the soul. In its first outreach it doesn't grasp God in so far as he is good, nor does it grasp God in so far as he is truth. It penetrates further, to the ground of God and then further still until it grasps God in his unity and in his desert. It grasps God in his wilderness and in his own ground.
>
> (quoted in O. Davies, *God Within*, Paulist Press, 1998, p. 51)

> Now see! So unified and simple is this 'fortress' in the soul ... that that noble power of which I have spoken is not worthy to penetrate this fortress even once for a single moment ... So simple and unified is the fortress and so beyond all manner and all powers that no power or manner, not even God, can ever find its way into it. In truth: God himself cannot enter there for a moment, and never has entered, in so far as he exists in the manner and nature of his Persons ... [I]f God is to enter there, then it will cost him all his divine names and the nature of his Persons; he must leave them outside its walls, if he wishes to enter inside. Rather, as he is in himself One ... he is neither Father, nor Son, nor Holy Spirit in this sense, and yet he is Something which is neither this nor that.
>
> (ibid., p. 52)

Now this is perhaps not the easiest language to grasp when we read it for the first time but do you get a sense of the radical images that Eckhart is using? When he speaks of the meeting between the human soul and God, this is one in which all ideas and beliefs are stripped away. The human soul reaches out to God, even beyond the idea of God as good or as truth, to meet with God's 'wilderness' or 'desert'. Similarly, if God is to meet with the human soul, God must remove all the concepts we have that relate to God. Even the idea of God as the three Persons of the Trinity, Father, Son and Holy Spirit, becomes like a set of clothes that God must remove in order to truly enter the fortress of our soul.

According to Eckhart, then, our encounter with God and our understanding of God is ultimately shrouded in mystery. It is a meeting in which our 'wilderness' meets with God's 'wilderness', a meeting that goes beyond understanding by any kind of theological doctrine or formula. Ultimately, the God we encounter is 'Something which is neither this nor that' and what we are left with is a sense of mystery and silence of this encounter rather than our ability to give it any kind of description.

You may not like what Eckhart seems to be saying here. But for some people who are in the car-park stage of transition, it may be reassuring to know that there have been Christian mystics and theologians who have suggested that the stripping away of ideas and beliefs about God can actually be part of the process of moving towards a deeper encounter with God. We may not know what to believe about God, but this uncertainty can form the basis for a silent meeting with the God who is really there, rather than the God that our theology tells us is there. From this apophatic point of view, what matters is not our ability to attach the right names or concepts to God but to be able to encounter the God who transcends and goes beyond any name or idea.

In fact for many people who pass through this kind of experience, what changes in the future is not simply *what* they believe but *how* they believe. Rather than returning to the same kind of certainty that characterises Evangelical discourse, they find themselves holding more lightly onto beliefs or theological concepts, recognising that there is a God who stands beyond all beliefs and ideas. Rather than staying with fixed systems of belief, they adopt ways of looking at the world that are more provisional and open to change in the light of subsequent experience. Spending time in the car park of doubt can be a difficult process, though, and in chapter five we'll think about some resources that may help us through it. Before then we need to think about some more specific challenges that may need to be faced in the process of moving on from Evangelical faith.

4
Facing the Darkness

There's no going back.
Ever.
There's no going back ten minutes,
let alone ten years.
Like the omelette, we are what we are,
because we've been through what we've been through.
Unmaking all that is too fiddly even for God.

So no, there's no going back,
no return to the Garden of Eden. It's barred to us.
And so to the next question:
Is there a way forward?
We've discovered God can't unmake omelettes,
but can he give the broken a future?
It's a question worth asking when you next pray . . .
(Simon Parke, *The One Minute Mystic*, Azure, 1999, p. 54)

In the last chapter we thought about the process of questioning or moving on from Evangelical faith as a journey. Not a particularly original metaphor but a helpful one, I think. And one thing about setting off on this journey is that once we've started out on it, we can never return to having the same faith that we had before the journey began.

In talking about this journey, there have been two basic ideas that keep cropping up. One is that if this journey takes us in the direction of a faith that is more true to our experience then this is a good thing which will lead us to spiritually and emotionally healthier lives. The other is that this journey can be a very challenging and emotionally demanding process which can involve feelings such as confusion, sadness, anger and loneliness or indeed varying levels of depression.

This dark-side of the journey is painful and one way in which we can think about it is in terms of a process of grieving. In fact, questioning or moving on from Evangelical faith can lead to some very tangible losses:

1. *A loss of community and structure.* Evangelical churches and organisations can be great at offering a wide variety of spiritual and social activities in which people can be involved. If we find that our questioning of Evangelical faith leads us ultimately to leave our particular church fellowship then this can involve a substantial change for our social networks and the way we spend our time. Putting it in these terms might sound a bit trivial but the actual process of reconstructing a social network and social life that was previously based on heavy church involvement can be slow and, at times, lonely.

2. *A loss of friendships.* In the last chapter, I suggested that questioning Evangelical beliefs can often be unwelcome in many churches. To raise honest questions can sometimes put real strains on friendships. And in situations where people ultimately decide to leave their church, it is not uncommon for them to discover that no longer attending church meetings also means losing touch with people who may previously have been good friends. This is not always the case – I have been fortunate through my own change of faith not to have lost any close friendships with people who are still involved in Evangelical churches and I am grateful to my friends for that. But I don't know how typical my experience is and suspect that 'loss of faith' all too often equates to 'loss of friendship' with those who still remain committed Evangelicals.

3. *A loss of partner.* A common cause of the breakdown of marriages and other close relationships is when one partner changes in a way that cannot be accommodated or handled within that relationship. This basic principle has a particular edge in the context of Evangelical relationships. When two Evangelical Christians get married, their faith is generally seen as the cornerstone of their relationship. Indeed Evangelical

churches unsurprisingly often encourage this emphasis through their marriage preparation classes or through the sermons that get preached at Evangelical weddings. Whilst this shared faith can obviously be a source of encouragement and intimacy between these partners, things can become much more problematic if one of the partners begins to feel less sure about this faith or feels that they may no longer even regard themselves as a Christian. This scenario can potentially be a make-or-break situation for that relationship. Can the person who has profound doubts and reservations about Evangelical faith maintain a healthy relationship with a partner who may still feel very committed to it? And can the person who still retains their Evangelical beliefs maintain a healthy relationship with their partner, even when that partner seems to be pursuing ideas or beliefs that appear quite wrong-headed from an Evangelical perspective? Yet another set of pressures occur if the partner who is questioning their Evangelical faith engages in a rebellion that was suppressed during years of righteous living as an adolescent (more on this shortly). Marriages and partnerships can and do survive these challenges. But not all of them do. And some people will find that one of the most profound losses in their movement away from Evangelical faith is the loss of their relationship with their partner or spouse.

4. *A sense of loss of God.* When I have spoken to some people about their movement away from a straightforward Evangelical faith, it's clear that one of the few things they were able to hold onto through this process of change was a sense of the presence or the reality of God. For many other people, though, this process can involve profound questions about who God is and in what sense God is present to us at all. Asking these questions can mean hanging round the car park of doubt where the sense of God's absence is often stronger than the sense of God's presence. And this sense of God's absence can be very tough, particularly if we are also grieving the loss of other relationships or parts of our lives as a result of the changes in our faith. C. S. Lewis wrote about this kind of experience very poignantly in *A Grief Observed*:

Meanwhile, where is God? This is one of the most disquieting symptoms. When you are happy, so happy that you have no sense of needing Him, so happy that you are tempted to feel His claims upon you as an interruption, if you remember yourself and turn to Him with gratitude and praise, you will be – or so it feels – welcomed with open arms. But go to Him when your need is desperate, when all other help is vain, and what do you find? A door slammed in your face, and a sound of bolting and double bolting on the inside. After that, silence. You may as well turn away. The longer you wait, the more emphatic the silence will become. There are no lights in the windows. It might be an empty house. Was it ever inhabited? It seemed so once. And that seeming was as strong as this. What can this mean? Why is He so present a commander in our time of prosperity and so very absent a help in time of trouble?

(Faber and Faber, 1961, pp. 7–8)

Although this experience of the absence or loss of God may, in time, be replaced by a new understanding of God's presence, this sense of the loss of God will need to be grieved as much as our other sources of grief.

Cataloguing these losses may make for rather depressing reading. In practice, though, if we are experiencing losses such as these it is best to begin to think about what these losses mean to us and how we might want, over time, to respond to them. Like the journey across Middle Earth, though, this is something to walk slowly through rather than to rush. In amidst these feelings of loss we might also have more positive feelings – feelings of relief, if we are moving on from a situation that has been damaging for us. Possibly some sense of peace of mind too, if we feel that we are beginning to reconnect with parts of our experience that have previously been lost to us or kept under wraps. The process of questioning or moving on from Evangelical faith is likely to be an emotionally ambivalent one, then, in which both emotional light and shadow is present at different times.

Clearly, though, the process of experiencing these kinds of

losses will leave us emotionally vulnerable. What is worse is that a loss of community, friends, partner or sense of God may mean that we find ourselves cut off from sources of support and consolation that would previously have been important to us at times of sadness, uncertainty or depression. Being able to spend time with people who accept and understand us will be very important in helping us through this painful time and in the next chapter we'll look at some of the ways in which that kind of support might be available to us.

In the rest of this chapter, though, I want to look at two further kinds of emotional struggle that can be involved with a process of change in our faith.

Grieving for what has never been

So far, we've looked at how a process of change in one's faith can lead to some tangible and important losses in our lives. For some people who have been Evangelical Christians as teenagers or young adults, there can be another less tangible set of losses to face. Cole Moreton describes this very well in his article 'The Curse of Faith' when he says:

> At this point I have to mention the extraordinary number of men in their thirties – and it is men who tell me about this stuff, so there may well be equal anecdotage for women – who have lived a good Christian life in earlier years, got married and been happy, only to find their equilibrium disturbed by growing thoughts of all the things they never did when they were young. Evangelical or Post-Evangelical men have their mid life crises sooner and with more ferocity than anyone else in the world, because we have fought so hard in keeping down the raging torrent of our teenage emotions that we are devastated when the dam finally bursts, 10, 15 or 20 years later.
>
> (Cole Moreton, 'The Curse of Faith', 2002, posted on www.fish.co.uk)

Now, it seems very much in vogue in our culture today to say that we have no regrets about our lives. But part of growing older for people who were Evangelicals as teenagers or young adults can often be an increasing feeling of having lost out on something. When others were out partying, or experimenting with 'sex, drugs and techno', Evangelical youngsters would be more likely to be found in prayer meetings or Bible study groups. Or when others tried out different relationships in early adulthood, or spent time travelling or living by themselves, many Evangelicals would find themselves married by their early to mid-twenties and possibly starting to have children. Part of this sense of loss is inevitably a 'grass is greener' syndrome but for many people faith can begin to seem more like a curse than a blessing, precisely because it has led to opportunities of youth being missed or passed over, opportunities that in some respects will never be available to us again. This can be particularly painful in our culture, in which youth and its perceived freedoms are held in such high esteem. To feel that we have missed out on the opportunities of youth can therefore feel to us like we may have missed the best part of life – and it's all downhill from here.

It's unsurprising, then, that this kind of sense of lost youth can lead to some savage early mid-life crises for people who have grown up in Evangelical churches. Douglas Coupland once coined the phrase 'rebellion postponement' to refer to people in their thirties who start dressing much younger or adopting unfortunate new haircuts as a delayed reaction to the rebellion they never had as teenagers (not that I can identify with this at all myself . . .). 'Rebellion postponement', Evangelical style, can find expression in much more unsettling ways than unfortunate fashion choices, though. Like it says in the Talking Heads' song, 'Once in a Lifetime':

> You may ask yourself, 'What is that beautiful house?'
> You may ask yourself, 'Where does that highway lead to?'
> You may ask yourself, 'Am I right, am I wrong?'
> You may say to yourself, 'My God! What have I done?'

An Evangelical-style early mid-life crisis can be accompanied by some deep and very uncomfortable doubts about the partner, profession, home or lifestyle we have chosen. Cole Moreton comments, for example, that 'a Christian bridegroom in his teens or early twenties is a time bomb waiting to happen, and woe betide the woman who marries him'. This is not a comment we might often expect to hear in Evangelical marriage preparation courses but its unfortunate truth is borne out in those marriages and relationships that never make it through the storms of the early mid-life crisis. Those who go through this crisis without major changes in their lives or relationships may still be haunted by daydreams of how their lives could have been different. Or by thoughts of opportunities that have been lost through earlier years of a devotion to a faith that has not ended up providing the certainties and securities that it once promised.

Recognising a sense of loss in relation to missed opportunities of youth is therefore another form of grief that we may have to face. What is more complicated about this kind of grief, though, is that we are not actually grieving for anything tangible or concrete. A few years ago a bereavement counsellor called Barbara Morley wrote an article called 'Grieving for what has never been' (*Contact: The Interdisciplinary Journal of Pastoral Studies*, 1996, vol. 120, pp. 22–5). In it she talked about how many forms of bereavement follow the loss of something tangible, like a partner, a child, a friend, a job, our health or even the prospect of the loss of our own lives. Whilst such losses can be tremendously painful, devastating even, there is also a sense that the loss has a clear focus. We know what we have lost. We can have memories of the lost person or object that may be painful but also potentially a source of strength or comfort. We may have rituals that help us commemorate the loss and our family and friends will be able to see clearly that we have experienced some form of loss.

By contrast, though, Morley notes another kind of loss which is far less tangible. This is the sense of loss of the person who would love to be in a married relationship but who remains single. Or the loss of the person who would love to be a parent but who comes to realise that they will never have children. Or the feelings of loss that someone with chronic mental or physical health problems has when they recognise that there are some aspects of life that they will never be able to experience or enjoy. A sense of lost youth is precisely this kind of feeling of loss.

Rather than a grieving for someone or something that we have had but subsequently lost, this other kind of grief is for something that we have never actually had.

Grieving for what we have never had, or for what has never been, can be a particularly complex and subtle process. We have no clear focus for our sense of loss other than our ideas or aspirations about what might have been. And because we have no real experience of what we have lost, we have no memories to return to or to work with as we grieve. There are no public rituals to commemorate the loss of something that has never been and there are less clear signals to others that we are experiencing this loss – unless we ourselves tell them. As a consequence it can sometimes be harder both for ourselves and those close to us to recognise that we are grieving and also more complex in trying to move through this process of grief.

An important part of grieving a sense of lost opportunities in youth is to reach the point of a realistic understanding of what we have lost. This might mean recognising a sense of loss of independence. A sense of loss of opportunity for different sexual or romantic experiences. A sense of missing out on parts of youth culture that we never got properly involved in because of our anxieties about their immorality. Or whatever it is for you. Facing this loss will mean facing up to things that really are lost and then facing the pain that we'll feel at these losses. Talking to other people about this sense of loss will also be important, as will facing up to our possible tendency to over-romanticise experiences that we've not actually had.

But we might also be able to re-evaluate our lives and think about what we could still change. Are there experiences that we missed out on in the past that are still open to us in some form? Part of the process of going through a period of grieving for the lost opportunities of youth may be a new wave of experimentation in which we try to discover afresh what we actually enjoy and value in life (which may turn out to be not exactly the same as what we thought we should enjoy as good Evangelical Christians).

Fundamentally, though, we may need to recognise that we have lost something in our past that cannot be retrieved. And in doing so we face the basic truth that loss is an integral part of human life.

Facing experiences of abuse in religious settings

In addition to a possible range of losses that we may face as we move on from Evangelical faith, some people may also find that they are carrying with them the effects of different forms of abuse that they have experienced in their Evangelical church or fellowship. Now, abuse, we often imagine, is something that happens elsewhere. We know that different forms of abuse take place in life but our natural assumption can often be that it doesn't happen in our neighbourhood (particularly if it is a 'nice' middle class one), or our work-place, or our family, and certainly not in our church. Part of the reason why some people begin to have serious doubts about their Evangelical faith or their church fellowship, however, is precisely because they have experienced some form of abuse within it.

It's worth me taking a moment to explain how I'm using the word 'abuse' here. When we hear the word 'abuse' now, we tend to associate it with the abuse of children, in particular with the physical or sexual abuse of children. There is a growing recognition, however, that in any relationship in which there is a difference in power between two people then there is the potential for abuse to take place. Books and articles have therefore been written about professionals, such as lawyers, doctors or psychiatrists, who abuse their clients or patients. News items occasionally break about the abuse of elderly residents by staff in care homes. And there is a growing number of people who are talking now about their experiences of abuse at the hands of church leaders.

Again, when we hear the word 'abuse' we tend to think about some form of physical harm or sexual assault being inflicted on someone – both of which are clearly damaging instances of abuse. A broader way of thinking about abuse, though, is to see it in terms of one person exploiting the power they have over someone else to meet their own needs or to protect their own interests. This exploitation can leave the weaker person in the relationship feeling trapped, used, devalued and powerless to change their situation. And importantly the vulnerable person can be left with the sense that their own feelings have been ignored or trashed. The person committing the abuse may not be aware in their own minds that they are acting abusively towards someone else. But whether the abuse is intended or not, such misuse of power over others can still be hugely damaging.

This broader way of thinking about abuse suggests that it is complex and may not always be easy for external observers to identify. Ruth Layzell, who has worked as a counsellor with people abused in religious settings, explains it in this way:

> Most spiritual abuse is not blatant or obvious. It is more subtle and pernicious, often appearing upright, blameless or godly to the uninformed observer, yet carrying with it the potential to devastate those on the receiving end. Its hidden-ness is one of the difficult things about it. But this potential for abuse to take place in religious contexts is beginning to be uncovered. Communities of faith face a challenge to examine their theology, structures and religious practices with a more constructively critical eye than has been the case in the past, when the assumption has often been that 'abuse cannot happen here' because we are serving God.
> (Ruth Layzell, 'Pastoral counselling with those who have experienced abuse in religious settings' in Gordon Lynch (ed.), *Clinical Counselling in Pastoral Settings*, Routledge, 1999, p. 107)

More is becoming known about instances when ministers or church leaders have physically or sexually abused children or adults within their care. But, with a broader understanding of abuse, we can see how a wider range of experiences also have an abusive element to them. For example:

- Sarah is struggling to conceive a baby. She goes for prayer ministry at her local church and one of the pastoral team uses their prayer as an opportunity to lecture Sarah about the dangers of feminism and how Sarah's lifestyle and career are hindering her ability to conceive.

- Sam explains to one of his church elders that he thinks he might be gay. This elder says that Sam should only remain in the church if he is prepared to seek deliverance ministry that would cast the demons of sexual immorality out from him.

- Julia is a curate working with her vicar John. Despite saying he has no problems with women's ministry, John never encourages Julia and only comments on her work when he has something negative to say. Her efforts to work harder to get a positive response from him have no effect other than leaving Julia feeling depressed and burnt out.

- June goes to a member of her pastoral team to talk about times when her husband hits her. She is quickly told to remember Jesus' command to forgive those who do wrong to us and receives prayer for the grace to be able to forgive her husband for his violence towards her.

- Mike, the senior minister of his church, uses his sermon one week to explain that those people who are questioning his plans for the church's future development have closed their hearts to God and are failing to hear what God is saying to them.

None of these events are the kind of thing that will ever make it into the newspapers as stories of religious abuse. But in each of these situations we can see how the more powerful person is using their power in the relationship to inflict a particular view or way of doing things on other people. In each of these situations, the more powerful person is not acting empathically and sensitively towards the more vulnerable person or group but is using their power to advance their own agenda regardless of the other's feelings, experiences and needs.

It may be that you have been on the receiving end of some form of abuse whilst you were involved in an Evangelical church. This may have been explicitly physical or sexual abuse, or it may have taken one of the more subtle forms of 'pastoral' abuse that we have just noted. If this is the case, then you may well have been left feeling hurt and possibly profoundly mistrustful of anything to do with organised religion. An important part of coming to terms with what this abuse has meant to you is to find another person or other people that you can talk to about what has happened. Being abused generally involves having our feelings, or our story, ignored by the person who is abusing us. If you can find someone who will listen carefully to you, accept you whatever you are feeling and help you to tell your own story of what was happening in that abusive situation then this may help you to begin to feel less oppressed by this experience. In many cases it might prove useful to talk this abuse through with someone who has particular skills such as a counsellor, and again we will think more about resources that can be helpful in these situations in the final chapter.

Can God give the broken a future?

Of all of the parts of this book, I have found this the hardest one to write. Anyone who is questioning or moving away from their Evangelical faith is likely to find this a painful process in some way. As we have seen, it can involve grieving over things that we have lost and for things that have never been. For some of us, it will involve the painful task of facing experiences in which we have been on the receiving end of abusive acts or relationships in the church. Writing about this reminds me of the parts of this process of change that I have found painful or that have been painful in the experience of other people that I've known.

Sometimes it might feel like all we are left with is the pain. And sometimes perhaps all we can usefully do is to feel our pain and not try to avoid it or minimise it. We cannot turn back the clock and regain what we have lost, nor can we avoid the painful things that may have happened to us in the past. The questions that remain are how we live with our pain in the present and whether we can have hope for our lives in the future. There are no easy answers and like the risen Jesus we may find that whatever our future, it will be one in which we still carry the scars of our suffering in some way. But also like him, we may find that these scars are no longer simply marks of pain

and death but marks that reassure us that even our past suffering can be carried and borne in the new lives that we are moving into.

5
Stories, People and God

So here we have reached the final chapter. Given that we've been thinking about faith as a journey then you might expect the last chapter of the book to be about where this journey ends up. What's the destination that we're heading to? Well, here's the thing. I don't know. I don't know where your journey of faith will take you and to be honest I don't know in every detail where mine will take me either. For some people this journey might mean leaving the Church altogether or exploring other religions. For others it might mean getting involved in a church with a Catholic, or Orthodox, or liberal flavour to it. For some people it might mean staying involved in Evangelical churches but being more open to discovering benefits from other traditions and perspectives. Moving on from a rigid Evangelical faith can lead people to follow lots of different directions and to suggest that there's any correct, one-size-fits-all, form of belief that people should adopt is just too simplistic.

So if there's no single destination for us to be working towards, how do we know that we're heading in the right direction? Perhaps often we won't and often we might feel that our steps are faltering or that making a choice between two different pathways is a hard and confusing process. But here are some basic principles that we might want to keep in mind to guide us along the way:

- Trust yourself.
- Listen to your feelings and try to understand them.
- Listen to God speaking to you through your experience.
- Listen to other people whom you trust and whom you know

are pursuing their own journey of faith with humility and integrity.

It's funny, but even now writing those words, I can hear the inner Evangelical that I still have in my head pursing his lips and making blowing noises. 'It's not right, it's not biblical,' he's saying, 'you're just encouraging some kind of vapid, touchy-feely spirituality.' Aside from being impressed that my inner Evangelical has the word 'vapid' in his vocabulary, I don't really take any notice of his views on this. Ultimately there isn't any simple formula by which we know God because, as mystics like Meister Eckhart realised, the true God stands above and beyond all theologies and formulas. The best we can do is to hear the truth of God by listening to our experience and to the wisdom of other people whom we trust and respect. In the end, I can't produce a final knock-down argument for what I've said here that would convince my inner Evangelical or anyone else. All I can do is say that I don't know of any other way, right now, by which it's possible to pursue a healthy and constructive spiritual life.

When I think about these basic principles, I also think how important it is to hold them all together. If we don't trust and value our own insights and experience, then we run the risk of being too dependent on other people's experiences and perspectives. And as we noted back in chapter two, if our spiritual lives fail to give adequate recognition to our true feelings or our important experiences then we're courting disaster for our emotional, physical and spiritual health. So we need to trust ourselves, to be prepared to think about our feelings and experiences and to imagine that what we discern through listening to our feelings and experiences can indeed be the expression of God's truth for us. At the same time, though, valuing our own feelings and perspectives without regard for others around us can be an expression of a spiritual and emotional narcissism that is damaging for all concerned. Trusting ourselves, whilst also being prepared to listen and reflect on the views of good friends or other helpful figures in our lives, represents a healthier balance on which to base our spiritual travelling.

I've come to believe that, in the end, it's not useful to evaluate our spiritual lives by the extent to which they conform to some kind of abstract theological or doctrinal check-list. Instead, it seems more helpful to me to focus on the fruits that this spiritual journey produces. Does it enable me to have some sense of peace, contentment and authenticity about my life? Does it allow me to feel like I really am being me? How does it affect my relationships with others? Does it enable me to feel proper respect, tolerance and concern for other people? Does it challenge me to carry on asking what principles such as truth and justice mean in today's world? Does it provide me with a sense of connection to the greater mystery of life in which I have been invited to take part? If you can answer yes with absolute confidence to all of these questions then you're certainly doing better than me and perhaps it's you that should be writing this book. I think for most of us, though, aspiring to be able to say yes to these questions provides a motivation for the spiritual journeys that lie ahead of us for the rest of our days.

So these are just some general thoughts about what it might mean to pursue a healthy spiritual life. In terms of the particular process of moving on from Evangelical faith, I think there are some things that can be important resources to help us along the way and we'll spend the rest of the chapter thinking about these now.

Telling your story

After this concluding chapter, you'll see that there are two interviews that I've also included as part of the book. The people I've interviewed – Jo Ind and Dave Tomlinson – have both made their own spiritual journeys from an Evangelical faith to a new form of Christian belief. Both of them have written books that traced this process of change and I think that both of them have some very interesting and useful things to say about what this experience is like.

I won't try and summarise those interviews here – you can read them for yourself – but there was one thing that came up in the interview with Jo that I wanted to mention at this point. Towards the end of the interview, she talked about the process of moving on from Evangelical faith that she'd seen both in her own experience and in that of some of her friends. She commented:

> I do have some friends who needed to move from their Evangelical experience for all the right reasons, but didn't do that step of questioning and reflecting. And they just went on with nothing, leaving a big question mark about that part of their life. Whereas for me it's very important for me to make sense of my story, to be able to say, 'I was an Evangelical Christian then because . . . And then that was going on for me . . . And then this happened and that happened, and I moved on and became this sort of person.' Almost to keep a track of myself. Not to have those cupboards of 'Oh my goodness, what happened to me, how could I have possibly done that?'

When Jo was talking about this, it seemed to me to illustrate a very important point about us needing to have stories that help us to make sense of our experience. Without going off into a big ramble around the terrain of narrative theory, it's fair to say that stories have an essential role in our lives. By telling stories we turn our raw experience into something that has an underlying point and meaning. This can be at the level of the everyday stories that we tell friends or partners – stories about getting stuck on the motorway, a nice evening out at the cinema, or about the person at the desk opposite us at work who we'd cheerfully strangle if this act were suddenly legalised. But on a larger scale we carry stories about ourselves that give us a deeper sense of identity of who we are as people. So the stories that I tell about my family background, about my educational experiences, about my previous relationships or about how I came to do the job that I now have, all contribute to my understanding of what it means to be this person called 'Gordon Lynch'.

Now, if religious faith is an important part of our lives then the story of how we came to faith and how that faith has developed over time is another example of a story that makes a fundamental contribution to our understanding of who we are as people. Part of the challenge that arises when that faith changes or evolves is that it means that we have to find a new story to make sense of what is happening in our spiritual lives. Finding this story can be very difficult when we're in the early stages of that change – particularly if we're hanging round the car park of doubt and all we know is that we've lost our bearings. Over time, though, we can begin to find a new language to express what's going on for us. We can begin to tell stories that aren't so much about our disillusionment with Evangelical faith or churches and which become more about what we've started to become excited about or energised by. This isn't a quick process – remember the idea of the gentle stroll across Middle Earth – but over months and years we can begin to find new stories that make sense of who we are or about the direction of those lives. Of course, those new stories are only provisional and they, in turn, will be challenged and replaced by yet more stories as our lives progress. But as we find ourselves more able to tell the story of how and why we came to move on from Evangelical faith, and what we find ourselves moving towards, so we can develop a positive sense of the direction of our spiritual lives.

In both of their interviews, Jo and Dave pay tribute to the positive contributions their Evangelical background made to their lives. By contrast, we saw just now in that quote from Jo, how previous Evangelical experiences may seem so alien or embarrassing in retrospect for some of us and that we might be tempted to ignore them or pretend that they were never a part of our lives. Certainly when I look back at some of the entries of my prayer journal from fifteen years ago, I find it hard to recognise that it was me that wrote some of those things. Part of the challenge of telling the stories of our lives in an honest way, though, is precisely being able to face up to those things from the past that seem odd or out of place and recognising that they have a part to play in who we are today. If I simply try to ignore my past, or brush it under the carpet of my psyche, then somehow that devalues it. Perhaps a greater sign of spiritual maturity – for those of us who've come from Evangelical back-grounds – is to be able to face those backgrounds honestly and be able to tell a fuller story of what was both good and bad about them.

As we saw in the last chapter, telling the story of movement on from Evangelical faith can be a painful process as we acknowledge losses that we've experienced on the way or possibly put into words experiences in which we have been abused. Finding ways of starting to tell those stories is something that we can do by ourselves – through writing journals or letters to ourselves or perhaps to God. It will be important, though, to be able to talk to other people about what is happening in our lives and this is the next important resource for change that we need to think about.

People

One of the most important resources we can draw on to help us through the process of significant change in our spiritual lives are people with whom we can honestly express our questions, doubts, our varying emotions and our emerging sense of where our lives might be heading. The process of change that we have explored in this book is a profoundly significant and challenging one for anyone to undertake and to attempt this journey purely on our own would be a hard path to go down.

There are different types of relationship that can be important to us through this process. It is important for us, first of all, to find good friendships in which we are accepted, understood, supported and challenged. Some writers are suggesting that in our contemporary world, friendships are becoming our most important relationships. Some people find that they are closer to their friends than their families. For some people, their closest friendships may outlast their marriages or other committed relationships. The importance of friendship is reiterated time and time again in popular culture – in TV programmes like *Friends* and *Sex in the City*, in films like *The Shawshank Redemption* or *My Best Friend's Wedding*. In fact, whilst our times seem to be characterised by a growing cynicism about the limitations of romantic love, there is a growing awareness amongst many people that it is our close friends who will be with us however our lives unfold.

If we are going through a time of significant spiritual change and development then our friendships can play a vital role in helping us through this experience. To be accepted by one's friends is important when we may be feeling uncertain about ourselves as we question or abandon previously held beliefs or lifestyles. To be understood by one's friends helps us to accept the validity of what we are feeling and what we are going through. To be supported by one's friends – or not abandoned by them – can lessen anxieties we might feel about letting ourselves, God or other people down by moving on from our Evangelical faith. To be challenged by our friends can help us to keep some perspective on ourselves and help us to see some of the things that might be damaging as we experiment with different forms of belief or different ways of living our lives. If we are in the fortunate position of having friends who know us well, who will stick with us, and offer us this kind of understanding, loving and challenging support then the pain and uncertainty of this spiritual transition will be somewhat eased.

As we've seen earlier, though, moving on from Evangelical faith can sadly also mean the loss of friendship with people who have previously been an important part of our lives. A decision to leave an Evangelical church or fellowship can sometimes leave broken friendships or just an increasing emotional gap with people that we have previously been close to. The ending, or the fading away, of such friendships may often have little malice associated with it (though sometimes that will be the case) but such endings are perhaps unsurprising if former friends find that they have less and less in common in terms of their beliefs or ways of looking at the world. These endings, if they occur, are sad and need in time to be grieved. Importantly, though, we may need to begin to find some new sources of support. This might be through attending another church, or church-based group, or perhaps through another set of people with no church connection at all. For some people it may be hard to find any such support in their local areas. In such instances, annual festivals like Greenbelt can be an important way of meeting with other people who are sharing a similar spiritual journey. Alternatively attending regular retreats can be another way of finding support. There are also internet discussion boards which allow for open discussion of religious doubts and questions (see e.g. www.shipoffools.com). Whilst finding support across the internet in this way has certain advantages and limitations, such virtual communities can play an important role for some people as they come to terms with the spiritual changes they are facing.

In addition to support from friendships or from other informal contact that we might have with people at festivals, on retreats or over the internet, it may also be important for us to have contact with someone who can offer us more structured or skilled help. Finding a spiritual director, for example, can be an important means of exploring what is happening in our spiritual lives in an open way. A constructive relationship with a spiritual director is one in which we feel understood, in which we sense that the spiritual director respects the integrity of our own individual spiritual journey and in which the spiritual director is able to offer us resources that enable us to explore our spiritual lives in new and creative ways. If you work with a spiritual director who offers none of these things, or with whom you feel pressured to follow a particular theological or spiritual line, you might want to consider whether this person is right for you and try to find another director. For some people, it will also be useful to make use of a professional counselling relationship whilst going through this process of change. Seeking counselling may be particularly appropriate if you are affected by some kind of abusive experience or relationship that you have previously had in your Evangelical fellowship, if your process of spiritual searching involves grief or depression that feels overwhelming, or indeed if you simply want a structured relationship in which you can talk through what's happening in your life. Now this may be a radical suggestion but I think that if you want to work with a counsellor then it is more important to work with someone who is well trained and whom you trust and are able to be open with, than to work with someone who is necessarily a Christian. There are some excellent counsellors around in various Christian networks and also others who are less skilled. Counselling is a specialised form of listening and not everyone, however good their intentions, is able to do a good job of it. Again, get a sense of whether you are respected, understood and helped in your counselling relationship and if not then think about possibly finding another counsellor. Suggestions on how to find counsellors or spiritual directors are included in the 'Further Resources' section at the end of the book.

God

A final resource for our spiritual journey that we need to consider in this chapter are new ways of thinking and speaking about God. Now a person's decision to move on from an Evangelical faith, or perhaps to leave an Evangelical church, can sometimes be seen quite negatively within that culture. Anyone who has spent much time in Evangelical churches will be familiar with phrases like 'backsliding' or 'loss of faith' which can sometimes get attached to people who make those kinds of changes in their life. But if we decide to move on from Evangelical faith are we really losing our religion?

Well, no, I don't think so. In fact, I don't think so for two reasons. Firstly there is reasonable evidence to suggest that many people who leave Evangelical faith do not give up Christian belief altogether and that God remains an important presence in their lives (see Alan Jamieson's book *A Churchless Faith* for more details on this). Secondly, and perhaps more controversially, I would also suggest that if someone abandons Evangelical faith because they cannot remain in it with a sense of integrity then they are actually moving closer to the God whose words of truth come to us through the raw material of our experience.

Losing my Evangelical faith does not necessarily mean losing my religion and it does not necessarily mean losing God. What it is likely to mean, however, is that I will need to find new ways of thinking and speaking about God that do justice to the meaning of God in my life. Finding this new language for God is really important and not simply a matter for those preoccupied with academic theology. For as I suggested back in chapter one, the language that we use about God will be part of a discourse that will shape how we see ourselves and the world more generally.

One of the important things to bear in mind with the words we use to describe God is that they are all metaphorical. No single word or concept captures the mystery of who God is and the words that we do use offer human analogies that help us to focus on particular characteristics within God. Hence we use concepts from human experience and associate these with God, which in the case of Evangelical discourse would often be God as 'Lord', 'King' or 'Father'. Speaking about God as 'Lord' or 'King' may be useful in terms of expressing our humility and deference in the face of ultimate truth and mystery but it can also carry connotations of a hierarchical order in which we have little value or autonomy. The metaphor of God as 'Father' may have more intimate associations for some people, for others it still sounds like it presents a patriarchal and hierarchical view of God's relationship with us, and we saw some of the problems with that kind of top-down view of faith back in chapter one.

Is it possible to change the record and to use some different metaphors for God? Well, yes of course it is. Clearly debates will rage about what kind of metaphors for God are appropriate within the boundaries of Christian belief but for those breaking out from more traditional Evangelical theologies a bit of experimentation here is probably no bad thing. What difference, for example, would it make to your spiritual journey if you thought of God as the ground of your being, the foundation of your existence who speaks to you through the truths of your unfolding experience? Or what difference would it make to think of God not so much as 'Father', 'Lord' and 'King', but as 'Mother', 'Lover' or 'Friend'? What difference would it make to think not so much in terms of following God's commands for your life as being engaged in a dance with God? Or what would it mean to think of God as being so beyond our comprehension that God becomes hidden in a cloud of unknowing, or within a light so bright that it appears to us to be like darkness?

As you read these alternative metaphors, some of them might have leapt out at you or resonated with you. Others might have just seemed a bit bonkers. The point here, again, is to find a language that does justice to the truths and spiritual realities that you can discern from your own experience. Perhaps the metaphors that are meaningful for you will end up being quite conventional in Christian terms. Perhaps they will be more radical or experimental. Ultimately, though, this is a process of finding a language for your faith that you can use with a sense of integrity and authenticity and in which you don't feel constrained to use words or concepts just to toe the party line in the particular church or group in which you are involved.

Some final thoughts

I remember once reading a book by a popular American writer on Christian spirituality (who I will not name for reasons of tact and discretion), in which he ended the introduction to his book by saying 'And remember that I love you.' Now this was obviously very kind of him and I'm sure very well meant on his part. But to be honest, it just felt rather sweet and sickly to me.

So in coming to a conclusion here, I thought it would probably be wiser and more tasteful not for me to declare my undying pastoral love for you. What I'd like to say is a bit more modest than that. This book has been borne out of my own experience of moving on from Evangelical faith. I have tried, though, not so much to tell my own story but to offer a wider framework within which my experience, and the experience of other people that I know, makes sense to me. My hope is that the framework that I've offered in this book is helpful to you to a lesser or greater extent. Wherever you are on your spiritual journey I hope you can find the desire, support and encouragement to keep looking for that which makes sense to you, that which inspires you and that which gives you a sense of connection to the deeper truths of our existence. For it is when we touch understanding, inspiration and mystery that we meet with God, and may we have many such meetings along the way. Amen.

Interview with Jo Ind

Jo Ind is an author and journalist, who lives with her husband in Birmingham. She is a member of a Church of England congregation in an inner-city part of Birmingham, in which she is the organist. She works as a journalist for the *Birmingham Post*, where she has a particular interest in writing about the different faith communities of the city. She is also an associate editor of *Third Way* magazine and contributes to the *Independent*, the *Guardian* and the *Church Times*.

In her first book, *Fat is a Spiritual Issue* (Continuum, 1993), Jo gave a very honest account of her experience of moving on from Evangelical Christianity through the process of addressing an eating disorder. Her latest book *Memories of Bliss* (SCM, 2003) explores the relationship between sexuality and spirituality.

I met up with Jo in January 2003 at a local café-bar in Birmingham to talk to her about her experiences of moving on from Evangelical Christianity and her current thoughts about God, sexuality and what Christian faith means to her.

GORDON: Can you say a bit about how you got involved in Evangelical churches, or how you became a Christian?

JO: Well, it was when I was aged 11. I didn't come from a Christian family – well, that was what I thought at the time, but since then I've come to define these things more loosely. But at the time I believed I didn't come from a Christian family. And I went to Christian Union at school because I was joining a club, not for any other reason really. I'd ended up being a form representative for the Christian Union just because each form had to have different representatives.

GORDON: And you didn't really have a sense of what the Christian Union was?

JO: No, I had absolutely no idea. There was a modern languages society and there were some other societies as well. I didn't know what modern languages meant and I didn't know what the Christian Union meant. But I went along and I was really surprised to hear people talk about God in ways that I'd never heard before. People saying things like 'God spoke to me'. It made me very curious and I thought that I'd quite like to find out if God would speak to me. So I started praying. And I was about 11, I was kneeling by the bed, and I had what I can only describe as a mystical experience. I was just overwhelmed by a sense of the presence of God and felt this presence, this love that is the source of the universe and is all around me and in me as well. And I thought 'Wow!' I was hooked. So I kept on praying and kept on having those kinds of experiences. At Christian Union, because it was an Evangelical kind of Christian Union, they said that I had become a Christian, and so that was how I began to conceptualise what was happening to me. What was offered to me was this Evangelical framework and that made a great deal of sense to me. So I believed that I'd had a Damascus road kind of conversion experience and that I was now a Christian, that Jesus had made this possible and that I was now going to heaven, and that my family was going to hell . . .

After that, I longed to go to St John's, Harborne which was the big Evangelical church that everyone seemed to go to in the Christian Union. And I wasn't allowed to go at first because my family thought I wasn't old enough to travel on the bus by myself. But when I was 13 I was eventually allowed to go. And that form of Bible-based Christianity was what formed me through my teenage years.

GORDON: In what ways was it formative for you?

JO: It was very clear. It was as simple as ABC. The gospel was always presented in very straightforward ways and when you're at that age that's what you need, that's what

I needed anyway. It was a very good way of beginning a faith journey, I think.

Also, my home life wasn't happy and I think that my faith was a way of surviving that. It gave me a very clear structure of belief that I could hold on to. It gave me a community of very close friends that I would pray with. And it gave me a sense that there was something bigger, there was something more. That there was a God who was holding me where my family weren't. So I think it offered me the security that should rightly have been mine as a teenager but wasn't, so it was very good for me in that way.

And I liked, also, knowing what to believe about things at a time when you're beginning to understand more about politics and those kinds of things. I liked having a very clear framework through which I could think about things and come to decisions. Otherwise I wouldn't have known what I thought about abortion or what I thought about socialism, or anything like that. I wouldn't have had any way of knowing what was right or not and one of the things that I liked about my faith was that it gave me this starting point for thinking about everything else.

GORDON: So a very kind of containing environment both emotionally and intellectually . . .

JO: Yes, very containing, that's a good word. And in a way expanding a little as well, because it gave me access to friendships outside of my school environment. And we would go on holidays organised by Christian youth organisations and so I got to know people of different ages and from different parts of the country. So through that narrow thing we had in common, Evangelical Christianity, I actually got to know a wider group of people than I might have done otherwise. So in some ways it was expanding. And also at an age when people are needing to define themselves against their parents, some people do it through alcohol or drugs, or different kinds of music, whereas my faith was my way of rebelling. And I don't regret that at all. My home wasn't safe enough for me to be the kind of person who stayed out all hours and that kind of thing. So to have a safe way of rebelling and defining myself against my parents was very good for me. I don't know how I would have survived at that time if I hadn't had my faith. I can't imagine.

GORDON: At what point did you start to feel different or more ambivalent, or when did you start questioning?

JO: I started to question it and have difficulties with it when I went to university. I had a range of different difficulties with it. I'll start with the intellectual difficulties. I studied English and Philosophy, which was a delicious combination. I wanted to study Philosophy because I wanted to know what truth was and I wanted to study English because I just loved literature so much. And I wanted to try to make sense of how those subjects related to each other. I was particularly curious about what language is and how it works. The conclusion that I came to was that meaning is not fixed in words, that there's something dynamic about the process of meaning. The meaning of a word is not something that's fixed in an absolute way. Words mean different things to different people in different contexts and at different times. They have slightly different resonances every time they are used. This is the mystery of meanings – that they evolve, that they constantly change. And coming to that view of language meant that it became very difficult for me to read the Bible in the way that I'd been taught in my teenage years, where you read the Bible to find out what God had actually meant when He said something at that time. Reading the Bible meant finding out what God meant so that we could then try to apply it to our lives. But through my studying at university, I started to think that there wasn't just one thing that God 'meant' and that even if God had meant that one thing then, then what did it mean today? And I could no longer look to the Bible in that definitive way that I had done before. I began to find new ways of reading the Bible and thinking about it that made sense to me, but it wasn't the Evangelical way of reading the Bible. This thinking about language challenged my notion of truth as well. I could no longer think of truth as finding the words that corresponded to the way the world was. Truth could not be like that because language was not like that. So I started to think of truth, as being Christ himself, as in 'I am the truth' rather than 'These words are the truth.' In other words, something is true if it evokes love, goodness, peace. Those are the true words.

GORDON: So that was a process of intellectual questioning that began to take you outside Evangelical ways of thinking?

JO: Yes, and the other pulls were ... Well, I found it very difficult to think that my friends who weren't Christians were going to hell. And the whole thing of not being allowed to take seriously the words and the truths of other people who weren't Christians, I just began to find repulsive. I couldn't accept this idea that there is just this one small way of looking at the world, when I was coming across people who had such different experiences and ways of thinking. I couldn't get my head round the idea that everything they had to say was rubbish because it wasn't what the Lord Jesus had said.

And another thing that went with that was that I found that Evangelical Christianity struggled to take the world and experience seriously. There isn't a sense of the whole world being charged with the grandeur of God, it's only the bits that Jesus has redeemed – the Church – that is charged with the grandeur of God. And I found that increasingly unattractive and untenable. And how that came to a head for me was through my having an eating disorder and discovering that my faith was actually making me more ill.

GORDON: Now from an Evangelical point of view that could seem a strange idea, because if you've got the right faith then surely everything should be okay. So can you explain more about how you found that your faith was unhealthy?

JO: When I say I had an eating disorder, I mean that I was completely out of control with my eating. I either starved myself or I stuffed myself, never in between. And I'd long since ceased to be able to eat when I was hungry and stop when I was satisfied. So I had a very unhealthy relationship to food and I think that Evangelical Christianity contributed to that. Because what I needed to do to get well was to trust my body and trust my appetites, and trust the goodness of my flesh. But I'd been taught not to trust my flesh and not to trust my appetites and to subdue them by my mind or the calorie counter. So the process of getting in touch with my body was actually counter to the whole spiritual discipline in which I'd been trained.

GORDON: So what had you picked up from the Evangelical tradition that put the body down or that made it harder to get in touch with the body?

JO: Well, this word 'flesh' was used quite a lot. You know, the desires of the flesh had to be subdued. The whole thing was about allowing the spirit to direct the mind and the body. That was the whole hierarchy that was presented to me. I don't know that I can pin that down to particular Bible verses or particular experiences. It was seeped into the whole thing. The idea of letting the body take the lead – ooh, not done!

GORDON: So how did you start to become more aware that this Evangelical ethos was something quite unhealthy for you?

JO: Well, it's always a complex process, isn't it? In a way, I'd say it was a process that probably lasted for about five years and so it's quite hard to condense and say how it works. And all these emotional and intellectual things went in parallel, you see, so they were all utterly interconnected.

I formed a Christian Union rebellion group – I carried on being part of the Christian Union – but in my third year at university I ran a Bible study group for the waifs and strays of the CU, for all the people who were finding it difficult, who were on the edge. So I did that with a friend who also found the CU difficult. And I went to live in the Catholic chaplaincy as well – the CU saw me as a bit of a spy in that situation and said 'are they Christians?' and that kind of thing. And the Catholics were equally suspicious of the CU. I guess what that did was to give me a vision of a different way of being Christian and through that I started to go to a Roman Catholic monastery in Sussex. That certainly gave me a different view of being Christian and I found it utterly attractive. Very, very exciting – including sexually – in ways that my head could not get hold of. In fact it took about ten years for me to get my head around that.

There was a crunch time with the Christian Union. This was in my second year at university when I went to an awful CU Bible study leaders' weekend in Leeds. It was just horrible. Something else that I found very unattractive about Evangelical Christianity at that time was that it was so emotionally thin. There was no depth or richness or nuance. It was all 'if you're happy and you know it, clap your hands'. Now that is an unfair caricature but it was insipid when I compared it to the mystery and the depth that I later discovered in the Roman Catholic Church. But I went on this Christian Union weekend away and I came home early because I just couldn't bear the smallness of the emotions and the smallness of the thinking, and I felt very angry about it. So I thought to myself, 'I am going to only accept things in my life that I believe. And if that doesn't seem to make sense to me, I'll just put them to one side.' Now that might seem like a very obvious thing for any rational person to do but there was this whole thing in the Christian Union that you *had* to believe certain things. If you couldn't believe that people who didn't believe in Jesus were going to hell then you were unsound and you had to somehow make yourself believe. Now that's a very difficult position to live with any integrity and I decided that my integrity was more important. My integrity was more important than *this* Bible – and by *this* Bible, I mean the Bible that the Christian Union was presenting to me. I decided to go with my integrity and that was a very, very scary thing to do. So, it's a long difficult process, but if I had to identify one point at which I decided to step outside the box it was that point. And I thought, 'If it works, if it makes sense, then I'll believe it and I'll go with it. And if it doesn't, then I won't.' Now whilst that was a very frightening step, there was also a relief about it as well and I've followed that decision ever since.

GORDON: And that can be very difficult from an Evangelical point of view because it can feel like you're putting your trust in your emotions or your experience, rather than in some kind of higher truth.

JO: Yes, it's very suspicious, it's very dodgy. And if you've spent years actively being taught not to trust your emotions or your self, then it's like turning your world upside down.

GORDON: So what did that feel like going through that?

JO: Well, it was very real. If I look back, I look back with a bit of a smile and think, 'Oh Jo, you were alive – you were very much alive dealing with all of those things, good on you girl.' You know, some people go to sleep and I wasn't doing that. But at times it was terrifying. And I think that the only thing that enabled me to take that step outside the box was the fact that I just *couldn't* stay where I was. I just couldn't. It was intellectually untenable. It was emotionally, utterly unattractive. The only thing it had to offer me was safety really but I just couldn't stay. I just wasn't well – my eating was just all over the place. Something had to change – I couldn't have carried on like that. When I stomped out of that CU weekend in Leeds, my rage gave me momentum and energy to change but I still had to make a decision. The anger gave me the energy but I still had to think and make a conscious choice.

GORDON: Can we talk a bit about your new book on sexuality? What led you to write it in the first place?

JO: It comes down to mystical experience again. I get turned on by things other than people. For example, when I was studying at university, I had an experience of being sexually aroused through my intellectual discovery. And when I was praying in the Catholic monastery I had experiences of being sexually aroused whilst doing that. Now this has led me to question all the ways in which society thinks about sex, which is you're either homosexual or heterosexual or in between. And that has never really resonated with me, to tell you the truth. I wanted to know what was going on in this experience, when I was turned on by God, as I would put it. And so I wrote the book to try to make sense of sexuality in the light of this experience.

I think the thing that I find particularly relevant is the sense of life pulsating through the whole of the universe. There's a bit in Colossians, 'In Him all things hold together'. This is the image of Christ as being the life that spurts through the whole of creation. This is very different to an Evangelical view of the world as being soiled, that God is in the Church and isn't anywhere else. And what I was really ready and hungry for was this idea of God's energy spurting through the whole of creation. Now that speaks to my sexuality – it turns me on. So I started to think about eroticism as being about God's energy, about Him drawing all people and all things to Himself. So when I'm turned on I'm sharing in God's work of drawing creation to Himself and this has become a central way in which I understand sexuality. This idea about sexuality of being about attraction between male and female (and sometimes about homosexual attraction) just seems thin, flat, it doesn't resonate with me or turn me on.

GORDON: So that's been a process of finding a way of making sense of sexuality that fits with your own experience and how has that process changed things for you in terms of how you see the world or relationships?

JO: Well, first of all, it's good to have a way of understanding sexuality that makes sense to me. I appreciate that everyone's sexuality is different and I know that some people can't relate at all to what I'm saying because they've never had an experience like it. I fully understand that, just as there are things about other people's sexuality that I really don't understand.

I also think that it's enabled me to be compassionate. Within Christianity, and not just there but within our whole culture, sex is generally understood as a penis entering a vagina. But if we understood sex as Christ drawing creation to himself then we have to question the status of that particular act. Vaginal intercourse is no longer centre stage. It has a place, it has importance, but it's not the pinnacle of sexuality. So what then do we use as our guiding principles in terms of how we relate to each other? I would say that the guiding principles that we use should be love yourself, love your neighbour and love the Lord your God, and on these three principles everything else hangs. That's what Christ said.

GORDON: Something that strikes me from what you're saying is that God then is a sexual being.

JO: But of course God's a sexual being! I mean what nonsense! How could we possibly be sexual if God wasn't sexual?! Of course, God's sexual! How could we have this dimension if it wasn't in the source of all being? I mean, what are we? Are we super-gods? Do we have something that God doesn't have?

GORDON: And I guess often in the Church sex is talked up and people say it's a good thing but the kind of underlying message is somewhat different to that really.

JO: Well, yes, I think I was taught that sex is good in the right context, which is something I agree with. I'm not saying it's a good thing everywhere, any day, any time. But whilst it is talked of as being good, it's often done in a very Laura Ashley way, in a kind of 'with the lights off, when you're married, three times a week' type of way. There's not much scope within Evangelical Christianity for other dimensions of sexuality, such as being attracted to people of the same sex, or being turned on through prayer. There's no scope for any juiciness, it's all very sanitised. And that's not a very sexy view of sex. It's just unattractive to me. This one man for one woman thing – there's no real way of making sense of our libidinous desires outside that framework. And that is just not true to experience at all. I mean, how could I possibly be turned on by my husband if I wasn't turned on by all the other things that I am turned on by. You know, it's all part of the same thing.

GORDON: It seems to me that across the Church, and I'm certainly thinking about Evangelical churches, there is a certain amount of anxiety about sexuality. And I think if there are issues that are going to split the Church in the foreseeable future, it's going to be issues around sexuality. What do you think that kind of anxiety is about?

JO: Well, in fairness, I think that our whole society has got a problem about sex, and I include myself in that, I'm not saying that I've found the Holy Grail or whatever. And yes, the Evangelical Church does have problems about sex. But you know, it doesn't have, to the best of my knowledge, problems about sexually transmitted diseases within its communities, there aren't big problems about unwanted teenage pregnancies in Evangelical communities, so it's got something right. So I wouldn't necessarily single the Evangelical Church out as having more problems with sex than anybody else. Sex is difficult. It's difficult to live, it's difficult to get your head round. And I don't see secular health workers, for example, as having got the hang of it where the Church hasn't. I don't see it like that at all. We're all struggling to make sense of it and it is one of those big imponderables like 'what is death?' You know, it's one of those sort of questions. So I would see the difficulties that the Evangelical Church has with sex in that context.

Now I do think that there is a problem in Evangelical Christianity about this business of squaring experience with the Word of God. And sexuality is a perfect example of where this tension shows itself up. Now I do have to say that I don't actually think that the Bible says the things about sex that Evangelical Christians believe the Bible says about sex. For example, I can't find anywhere in the Bible where it says that you shouldn't have vaginal intercourse outside of marriage. I can't see that idea was rooted in the Bible. But sexuality really is an area where the clash between what people think the Bible says about sex and their experience just hit each other head on.

GORDON: One final thing that I wanted to ask you about was where you are now in terms of your own personal spirituality? Because one of the things that interests me is that for some people who've been through the process of questioning that you've been through, they'd end up quite a long way away from the Church or not want to engage with Christianity any more. But Christian faith is still obviously really important to you.

JO: Yes, it is. I must admit I am a little bit impatient with people who throw all faith out of the window because they've had a bad time as Evangelical Christians. Now I understand it, I know what happens, but I find it a little bit lazy to tell you the truth. I'm not the kind of person who can do that because I'm a person who has to examine things. I do have some friends who needed to move from their Evangelical experience for all the right reasons but didn't do that step of questioning and reflecting. And they just went on with nothing, leaving a big question mark about that part of their life. Whereas for me it's very important for me to make sense of my story, to be able to say, 'I was an Evangelical Christian then because . . . And then that was going on for me . . . And then this happened and that happened and I moved on and became this sort of person.' Almost to keep a track of myself. Not to have those cupboards of 'Oh my goodness, what happened to me, how could I have possibly done that?' And it be something that you could never think about and were just embarrassed about. I can be proud of the faith that I did have as a teenager and I can see what it gave me, at the same time as understanding why it was very important to move on from there.

So, where am I now? If I was to describe what sort of Christian I am, I would say that I am a practical Christian. Because I think that the most important thing for me is the 'it's by the fruits you shall know it' kind of belief. And in a way I guess that I've never moved on from that point when I came back from that CU meeting and said to myself, 'I'm only going to believe this if I can really take hold of it and make sense of my lived experience through it.' Consequently, I'm agnostic about an awful lot of things – maybe Christian agnostic is a good way to describe me as well.

I do need to have some way of making sense of the

sublime, the divine, the nebulous. I need to have some framework, some tradition, some discipline in which to practise. I'm not at all satisfied by or interested in this postmodern supermarket sort of approach where you do a bit of yoga here and sing a carol there. Not because I think we have to swallow traditions wholesale. I'm the last person to believe that. But it's because I believe that we cannot find who God is on our own. It has to be part of a community. And for all that we have to live in the present moment, I also don't believe that the now has got all the answers either. When we have this rich tradition of people through the centuries who have prayed, and studied, and followed God, if we've got any sense we'll listen to that and digest it. So I choose to worship as part of the Christian community. I have a sneaky suspicion that if I had been born into a Hindu culture then I would choose to practise as a Hindu. There is no reason for me to convert to any other religion because you can find truth where you are, in the culture and with the stories that you've been given. And there's a tremendous advantage in being part of a tradition into which you've been born and into which your parents and grandparents and so on were born. So I'm happy to say that I belong to the Church of England in Birmingham and this is where I practise. At my church, the vicar's central message is that whoever you are and whatever you are, you are loved by God. And that's the gospel for me, that's what it means, that's what faith is about.

Interview with Dave Tomlinson

Dave Tomlinson has an interesting history as a church leader and writer. Dave grew up in Merseyside and attended a Brethren church through his childhood. He later became involved in the Charismatic movement and by his early twenties was involved in leading a new independent Charismatic church with his wife, Pat. For a number of years, Dave was a leading figure in the emerging house church movement, and for a number of years was a leader of a network of such churches.

From the late 1980s, though, Dave became more detached from the house church movement and over time gave up his leadership role within it. With Pat, he helped to form a new group, Holy Joes, which met in a South London pub and provided a forum for people who would not otherwise feel comfortable or welcome in church settings. Through the 1990s, Dave developed closer links with the Church of England in London and this over time led to him being ordained as an Anglican priest and he is now the vicar of St Luke's, Holloway.

A well-known speaker at events such as the Greenbelt Festival, Dave is perhaps most widely known for his book *The Post-Evangelical* (Triangle, 1995) which became an important text for many people who were struggling with their involvement in Evangelical churches. I met up with Dave in his North London vicarage in February 2003 to talk to him about how he saw *The Post-Evangelical* now and about his own experience of spiritual change and growth.

GORDON: I wanted to talk first of all about your book *The*

Post-Evangelical. It's nearly ten years since it was first published and I think it's been a really important book in
terms of providing a language and a framework for people
who are questioning their Evangelical faith. Can you tell
me what led you to write it originally?

DAVE: Well, it's interesting that it's had such a long shelf
life – it's just had a fifth print – and that it had such a big
positive reaction. I mean, it obviously had a critical reaction which was to be expected. But the fact that it had
such a big positive reaction was a surprise to me because
I wrote it as a pastoral response to the people that I
was encountering at the time, but that I imagined was a
relatively small group. These were people with an Evangelical background, generally in their twenties and early
thirties, who were disillusioned with that Evangelical faith
but wanted to find a way of carrying on their spiritual
journey. And although you wouldn't have guessed it from
some of the criticism it received, I wrote it to say that I
didn't think that pure liberalism was the way forward.
I was trying to suggest a third way because, as I said in
the book, theological liberalism is really just the other side
of the coin to Evangelicalism.

So, it was written as a pastoral response to these sort
of people to say there is a way forward – there are probably many ways forward and this isn't *the* way, but these
are some thoughts you might find helpful. The surprise,
though, was the huge amount of correspondence that I
got when it was published. I've got a file with hundreds
of letters from people, many of whom didn't fit this target
group. Many of them were older and probably culturally
more conservative than the group I had in mind when
writing it. And these were people who probably looked
like satisfied customers in Evangelical churches but who
had obviously carried a whole raft of doubts and questions that they hadn't previously felt able to voice. A lot
of them were saying, you know, 'I've thought these things
for years' or 'At last, you've put a name to this'. And I
do think that I was naming something that was already
there, rather than creating something new. But giving a

name to something can be a very empowering thing
because it can help you to realise that you're not alone in
how you're feeling.

GORDON: So when you say it was a pastoral book, was your
aim really that it might keep people in the Church who
might otherwise end up moving out of it?

DAVE: I suppose when I wrote it I was pretty much on the
fringes of the Church myself, really. I wasn't attending a
church regularly on a Sunday. I was running Holy Joes,
having stepped out of the house church movement and
the career that I'd had in that. I was certainly writing it
to keep people in the faith and I suppose in the 'Church'
in the big sense of the word. But I was already
immersed in Holy Joes which was a pastoral project in
itself, really, because it recognised that many people don't
feel easy in the Church or can't fit in but need some kind
of community. Because I do believe that at the end of the
day Christianity is not an individualistic faith. I think
Christianity is essentially communal, which is not to say
that you can't exist as a Christian in isolation, but I do
think that there is something about the corporate dimension of living the Christian faith which is very important.

So yes, I was coming across so many people who were
dropping out of the Church. I still do, in my work as a
parish priest. These are people who have had church up-
bringings, who've been Evangelical Christians, but who
are now out of it. There are lots of people who drop out.
I think many of them needn't have dropped out of faith,
and lots of them never wanted to, but they just found that
the church wasn't helpful for all sorts of reasons, in some
cases it was damaging and to say the least unedifying.

GORDON: And in your writing, and when I hear you speak,
your own commitment to Christian faith is very clear and
it's obvious that you think that staying in touch with the
Christian tradition is genuinely valuable for people. Can
you say more about what you think is valuable about it?

DAVE: I'd have to say that I'm not taking that position in
the sense of saying 'This alone is the way'. I believe that
God is bigger than Christianity and therefore I'm very

comfortable with the idea that God is leading people in many other ways. And as to what is entirely valid, I don't feel I have to comment on that because I'm not God! But I do believe that God speaks to people in many ways in other faiths and none. But, if I'm brutally honest I have to say I've stuck with Christianity because it's what I grew up with. You know, there is a sort of historical heritage there. But also having looked at other options, I still feel that this is the comfortable way forward for me, this is the way that I feel happy with. And my own view of Christianity has expanded – partly through understanding better the actual historical tradition of Christianity – and this has given me a sense of Christian faith that is more accommodating than other forms that would lead people (including myself) to leave the Church.

In my deepest and darkest hours of questioning, I do as much as anyone feel that perhaps this is just a load of cobblers. Perhaps there isn't anything more than this life. You know, I bury lots of people these days and some-times you think, 'Well maybe, that is all there is.' Ultimately I don't actually believe that and I don't spend much of my life in those deep, dark hours. But even when I'm at that point, I still feel I'm contented with being the kind of person that Christianity has made me, even if this life is all that there is. So I feel that the values that it has given me, the life that it has given me, the experience of community that I have through it, are all positive. And if in the very last hour of my life I suddenly found that it was all untrue, I wouldn't feel any great regret because I'd feel that this was as good a way to live a life as you can.

GORDON: Why do you think *The Post-Evangelical* provoked such strong responses, both positive and negative, from people?

DAVE: I'd like to say that it was because I'm a really clever person and that I'd spotted a gap in the market – but I think it was an accident really. I think that, whilst I was voicing my own authentic journey, I also inadvertently managed to voice something that was far more widespread than most people realised. I think that some of the vehemence in the attacks that I got – some of which were so over the top – was clearly coming from a sense of insecurity, that there were deep rumblings here. You know, within a few months of the book coming out, *Third Way*, which would be considered one of the more thoughtful Evangelical journals, did a survey in which 25% of their readers had identified themselves as post-Evangelical. This was really pretty remarkable given that the idea had only just been launched. Now you can imagine that the keepers of the establishment who read that would feel a little shaky. It wasn't that I had created this situation. I named it and voiced it, and in doing that I uncovered just how widespread some of those feelings and views were. And it's understandable that if it is that widespread then there are a lot of people who are going to say 'Thank you, at last someone has said this' and that there are other people who are going to feel quite threatened by that and who are going to try to pull the boat back in again.

It was interesting that a lot of conversations that I've had since writing the book are with people who aren't from an Evangelical background, but have the same experience. They might be post-Catholics, or even post-liberals, or whatever. I think that what I described and identified is within the Evangelical context but it's also something that is much bigger than that. It's to do with a cultural shift away from modernity which has dislodged a lot of people away from the status quo in different traditions in the Church. So you can find yourself amongst people with very different Christian backgrounds but who share a similar journey of unease with absolutism or the certainties of whichever tradition it is and wanting to draw on strengths across those traditions. I mean, in my own experience, my spiritual trajectory has been in a more Anglo-Catholic direction and it's surprising how many Evangelicals (who wouldn't even call themselves post-Evangelicals) now live with aspects of Catholic spirituality that they wouldn't have been seen dead with a few years ago. Likewise in Catholicism, you find people who are virtually Evangelicals, who want to proclaim their faith and the Charismatic movement is huge in the Catholic Church. So there is this sense of a kind of melting pot going on. And the old guard might be trying to force people back into the trenches to fight for the old fixed positions, but really that's hopeless. I think that there will always be a market for that but many people now don't want to be defined by, or limited by the traditions of the past as tribal, sectarian kind of positions.

GORDON: Another book that's been published more recently that reminds me very much of *The Post-Evangelical* is Alan Jamieson's *A Churchless Faith*. Many of the reasons that Alan Jamieson describes for why people leave Evangelical churches are the same issues that you were describing back in *The Post-Evangelical*. Do you think anything much has changed in Evangelical churches since you wrote *The Post-Evangelical*?

DAVE: That's a very good question and I don't know if I'm really equipped to answer it. Certainly the term 'post-Evangelical' has now entered the language of people with that kind of background. You come across people who describe themselves as 'post-Evangelical' who would never have heard of me or my book. And I've seen church leaders describe their churches as post-Evangelical too. I do think that Evangelical churches have changed. I've had some very positive contact with people who are Vineyard pastors – I would never have expected that. And people who would not necessarily want to be identified with me publicly who have communicated in private about how much they agree with what I'm saying – which is interesting too. But I do think things are changing. People don't want to be locked into things. People might feel most comfortable in Evangelical churches at the moment but they don't want to defend a sectarian Evangelicalism any more. So I think there's a process of glasnost going on. Critics would probably see that as a sign of an insidious movement of liberalism. But I think often it starts with people's social attitudes, and their attitudes towards the Church sub-culture as well, rather than with theological issues as such. But I think it is a process that does have inevitable theological outcomes. Once people, for example, find that they know gay people and that they actually have some sympathy with where they're coming from, although they might be trying to hold tenaciously to a conservative theological view on homosexuality, in reality there's going to be an underlying momentum of change taking place in their beliefs.

GORDON: So is what you're describing a grassroots process of change? And if so, do you see Evangelical church leaders as trying to catch up with this process?

DAVE: Yes, I think so. In some cases, there are church leaders who are further down the road than their congregations, so there are situations like that. But I think that church leaders have sadly had the inclination to shield people from the nasty, hard questions of academic theology and I think that's been a very big mistake. In fact, in pastoral terms, it's catastrophic further down the road. One of the things I was saying in *The Post-Evangelical* is that the post-Evangelical impulse very often begins at a cultural level, with a feeling of disengagement from a lot of the Evangelical sub-culture. In the old days people might have said that attitude was 'worldly' because it's being influenced by the wider culture. But that wider culture becomes too pressing for people and that has an effect on moral and ethical attitudes and outlook, and eventually that has to come down to the business of theology. But often, theological attitudes, however badly thought out, are like comfort blankets. And however grown up people might be in other ways, they can find it quite hard to change these theological beliefs. So that process can take quite a while but inevitably those questions have to be faced.

GORDON: Another thing that you were talking about in *The Post-Evangelical* and that Alan Jamieson talks about as well in *A Churchless Faith* is the need for church communities that can allow a broad range of different kinds of spiritual development. Now you've been involved in church leadership in a range of different settings, what kind of styles of church leadership are needed to create those kinds of church communities?

DAVE: Well, I suppose this is why I feel quite comfortable in the Church of England. The Church of England contains both extreme fundamentalism and extreme liberalism. In a given church you might find something that is very narrow in its own particular way but the overall breadth of Anglicanism is something that I feel very comfortable with. There's space to explore and grow, which compares very favourably with the sort of church background I had before that in which you felt that if you stepped half a yard either way, then you were in danger of falling into heresy.

On the level of individual church, I look at a church like St Luke's where I'm the vicar and I think that the criteria for membership are very broad. I do believe in people belonging before believing. There are people who I'm sure feel that they belong at St Luke's who aren't sure what they believe yet and certainly couldn't tick all the right boxes according to some people's criteria. But I think that's a journey and people can work that out. And on a given issue in church life you would probably find a whole range of views at St Luke's and you don't have to sign up to a particular package of doctrinal or theological beliefs. So I think that the kind of church leadership that we need today is one that allows for an enormous breadth and which is more journey-oriented rather than being about signing up to a particular doctrinal agenda. It's about being tolerant of other people's beliefs and lifestyles, whilst still holding confidently to the core of the Christian faith. I think there's a huge difference between confidence and certainty. If a church is going to have the cohesion to go anywhere, then there does need to be some sort of core commitment. But it's not a commitment that should be imposed on people but one which invites them on their own journey of exploration and which affirms people wherever they are on that particular journey. I think that the sort of church leadership that we need is the sort of leadership which allows for much more debate and questioning. There are some people who, from time to time, will interrupt and question me in the middle of my sermons and I relish that. I wish more people would do that. Within the context of the life of the church, leaders need to provide forums where people can really debate and discuss issues. But there still aren't many places where people can put their hands up and say 'Hang on a minute, I'm not too sure about this' or could question what's being said. There are plenty of churches where people can ask questions to clarify what's being said but far fewer where you can really question what is being said. So basically, church leadership needs to develop in the skills of facilitation. Church leaders need to be facilitators of a discussion and spiritual guides, rather than the sort of didactic directors who lay down the criteria and say 'Tick these boxes and sign up to this or you can't be here'. It's much more about providing resources for people's development.

GORDON: Now that sounds like quite a difficult balance between encouraging people to pursue their own paths at the same time as having a clear sense of your own Christian faith and identity. Do you find it hard to maintain that balance at times?

DAVE: Yes, I do find it hard at times. Because I know that on all sorts of issues I may be going through similar questions to other people in the church. And I think that another important quality in leadership in the church today is honesty. If one is going through the same questions and doubts, one needs to have the courage to say so. There can be a fear of confusing people but I think it's actually a really helpful thing to do. I mean we need this in politics – we'd all like some politicians who would say, 'I don't know, I'm not sure.' But they're not allowed to do that. And I think church leaders haven't been allowed to do that. But I think it is important to be honest, even if it's difficult to do that.

The sort of confidence in Christian faith that I'm talking about is born out of a process of going through doubts and questions. And if you've been through that process then you know that complex questions can potentially lead to a range of equally valid answers. But that shouldn't stop you from giving your own perspective, as long as you're honest about where you're coming from.

GORDON: And I guess sometimes it can be very hard in Evangelical churches to say what you really think about things, perhaps for the leaders as much as anyone else. Like you were saying earlier about the church leaders who told you in private that they agreed with what you said but who weren't comfortable saying that in public.

DAVE: Well, there's an example of such a church leader in *The Post-Evangelical*. There's a story there about a Baptist minister that I spent several hours talking with whilst he poured out doubt upon doubt and question upon question. Now if he'd voiced any of those things in the large and successful Baptist church he was leading then I think that his position would have become untenable. And the sad thing is that he had to travel quite a distance to talk to me, when he didn't know me very well, to be able to pour this out because he had no support around him where he was and because there was such insecurity around this. Eventually he did leave the ministry and I'm sad that he had to leave what had been a calling because it wasn't possible to reconcile his questioning with the expectations of the congregation that he was working with. So I think that there's quite a lot of pain around on the part of some church leaders. I know, for example, from private conversations, of Evangelical church leaders who are gay. Now how could they possibly admit to that in an environment in which homosexuality is often demonised? And some people who have come out in those situations have gone through some very painful experiences. So it's difficult when churches have such hard and rigid views that you either have to sign up to or you become some kind of pariah and face all kinds of problems.

GORDON: And church leaders really do need support in that kind of situation.

DAVE: Well, yes, I think that church leaders do need places in which they can be honest. Fraternal relationships aren't always the best for that, particularly if you're in a group where people all see it in the same way. But as *The Post-Evangelical* demonstrated, there are lots more people going through these kinds of questions than there appears to be on the surface.

I think that church leaders are becoming increasingly aware of the need for spiritual direction, of someone that they can go to who they can talk to in confidence and get some support and guidance. I personally think that every church leader should have a spiritual director – I mean, you can call them mentors or coaches, or whatever, but we need those kinds of relationships.

GORDON: We've talked about the range of people who identified strongly with *The Post-Evangelical* when it was published. But what's happened to those post-Evangelicals in the years since your book was published? Have they stayed in the Church?

DAVE: Yes, I think lots have. I think when the book first came out, there were some people who said to me that they thought we should get some kind of movement underway. But I always maintained that I didn't see myself as launching a movement as such but saw being 'post-Evangelical' as a stepping stone on a journey. Now that journey might involve people staying in their Evangelical churches but feeling more confident in themselves and hopefully broadening the environments in which they feel more confident. And I think that has happened for some people. For other people it might be a stepping stone into some other tradition in the Church. I know people who have begun to explore Catholic or Orthodox spirituality – aspects of Christian tradition which they hadn't been introduced to in the past but which they find helpful or beneficial. I think that there are some who have felt that it just highlighted how depressing the Church is and who have left the Church altogether. And as someone who is committed to the Church, I'm sad that that happens. But I understand why it happens and I don't think it's the end of the world, because I don't think that God is contained in the Church and I think that God is still in their lives, just as God is in the lives of people who have never been to church. So that's not the end of the world. But I do have a vested interest, because I think there ought to be a way forward.

But I find it terribly, terribly hard when people ask me, as they constantly do, 'Do you know of a church in Little X or Greater Y that I could go to?' And I don't know. Perhaps the one thing that I think might be helpful would be if some kind of informal network emerges where people can find others like them. I think that perhaps that's something that maybe I should have helped to happen and maybe that should happen.

But there are some places. Greenbelt is a classic example of a post-Evangelical gathering point and I meet people there every year who say that it's going there that helps them to keep going. I know some people who treat it as their church. It is their one tenuous connection with the church community which they have once a year. Other people find that they can cope with some of the crap that they do put up with in the Church because there is this wider network out there of people who share the same kind of thinking.

We're in a time of great change and transition. I expect there to be a fair amount of jiggling around, if you know what I mean, of people trying out other churches that they've never been to before and perhaps finding that helpful. Or perhaps taking a break from church and sometimes for sanity's sake alone that's necessary. But I do think that support networks are important and the more of those that develop the better.

GORDON: So, although a lot of people have identified with the idea of being 'post-Evangelical', many of these people still feel quite isolated in their churches?

DAVE: Yes, I think lots of them do. I think that naming 'post-Evangelicalism' has helped because people have found that they are not alone and that there are other people who feel the same way as them. But undoubtedly there are people who do feel isolated, that's for sure. And there's no easy answer to that without saying you have to move here or there, which is silly really. But I hope that the outcome of *The Post-Evangelical* would be that people try to engage in a useful and constructive way with the Church. But I recognise that's easier for me to say than others because I have some influence and opportunities as a leader of a church and I can set out my stall and do my thing. Whereas for a lot of people they're not empowered to be able to do that. But I hope that people can find a 'second innocence' which goes beyond cynicism and criticism and which doesn't destroy the doubts and questions but takes them forward in a constructive way. I mean I have re-engaged with the Church. I'm a vicar, for goodness sake, who would have thought of that? I've engaged with a tradition that at one time in the past I would have spurned and I've found that tradition to be nourishing. I've had to find my own ways of interpreting it and re-configure how it works in my life but I'm nevertheless drawing on some very deep wells and I find that tremendously nourishing. So I suppose what I want to do out of a pastoral concern is to help people, say, to re-engage with the Bible rather than tossing it aside and saying 'I can't do anything with that', or to re-engage with prayer rather than being disillusioned for ever as to why God doesn't answer in some kind of simplistic way. And to do this by drawing on rich traditions which always need re-interpreting and re-applying but which contain great potential.

GORDON: As you've said, you've been through some quite significant changes since the days when you were a leader of a network of house churches and probably wouldn't have imagined that you'd be here today as a vicar in an Anglican parish. What's that process of change been like for you?

DAVE: I suppose the fact that I wrote *The Post-Evangelical* as a way of trying to keep people in the fold was a mark of something that was going on in me too at that time.

GORDON: So you were trying to keep yourself in the Church too?

DAVE: Yes, that's right. I mean I wrote it at a time of serious theological study for myself which was my way of trying to grapple with what I believed and to see if there was something that I could find that I would feel comfortable with. And *The Post-Evangelical* was really about biblical interpretation, because I didn't think I could be a Christian and throw the Bible away. Christianity is a faith of the book. So I was going to keep on this pathway, I was going to find a way of dealing with the Bible. And, for me, looking at the whole world of contemporary hermeneutics was very helpful. I discovered that there were so many different ways of approaching the Bible and interpreting it. Helping people to find fresh ways of reading the Bible is something that I feel really quite passionate about – helping people to read the Bible in ways that are nourishing and which don't have to buy into all those ideologies about inerrancy and that kind of stuff.

And prayer is something else that I've had to re-interpret. As an Anglican priest you are supposed to say Daily Office and that wasn't really the pattern that I was accustomed to in the past. But I've actually found that incredibly helpful. In the past, in the Evangelical world that I'd lived in you were supposed to pray, but how the hell do you do it? Where do you start? Where do you finish? What do you do? It had always been a failure to me, as I think it is for a lot of people. But I've now found that working with an ancient structure of prayer – for me, the Benedictine tradition of daily prayers – has been really helpful. I've started to look at it all in a different way. Liturgical repetition becomes a kind of mantra, really. One of the problems of coming from an Evangelical tradition is that you feel that you've got to *mean* everything and to be able to use liturgical patterns as a way of getting beyond that is helpful. In fact, one of the big gaps in the *The Post-Evangelical* was spirituality and if I was writing it now I would definitely want to have that as part of it.

GORDON: So this has been a really interesting journey that you've been on – and what's kept you on track through it? How have you been sure that you've been taking the right paths?

DAVE: Oh, I certainly haven't been sure! You know, I've had all sorts of doubts and questions about it. But the truth is that journey started way back in that house church period. The people who were around me at the time then were constantly looking askance at me, wondering which rug I was going to pull out from under their feet next. So when I was really in the midst of being a house church leader and all the rest of it, I had so many doubts and questions that I voiced at leaders' gatherings. But what they wanted me to do was to repeat the old mantras, to say the old reassuring things, and I couldn't do that because I had all these doubts and questions. So you know the journey goes way back there. And I did have these strange thoughts even then that I might one day end up as an Anglican – which just seemed bizarre at the time – but I did have those thoughts even then.

Looking back it feels like a seamless journey. It feels like I've just taken the next step and the next step and the next step. At the time, each step felt like the obvious step to take. But I didn't have this clearly packaged vision of 'This is where I need to be', and I'm as surprised as anyone to find myself where I am today.

GORDON: We've talked today, then, a bit about the process of change that you've been through and I imagine that people reading this book will be going through their own changes too. What would you say to people who are in the middle of that process?

DAVE: Well, I guess one of the difficulties can be that none of us knows how many security blankets we're really clinging to. And I want to say, 'Let go and just explore – believe that God is bigger than your past experience or than the parameters of the particular part of the Church that you've come from. Just have a go and explore – have a look around the place.'

The problem is that we're living in one room in a mansion, I think that's how it is. And I do think that the Evangelical part of the Church is in a mansion – you know, it's part of God's house and it would be disingenuous of me not to acknowledge how much I owe to my Evangelical background. It's given me so much, I am where I am today because that's where I started off. But it's only one room in the house, you know, and there are so many rooms. So get out there and explore and have a look around the place. Maybe you'll feel comfortable with things that I don't, but that's fine. Really what I want to say is that within this rich household there are so many possibilities – so don't give up too quickly. This particular room might not be to your taste but others may well be, so don't give up, keep exploring. Try to find travelling companions who'll share that journey with you as well. Because even in the most conservative church environment, if you have one or two people who you share a kindred spirit with then you can keep on going. It's harder trying to do it all alone. And if you can't find it in your own church, then maybe look for it outside and beyond, maybe once a year at Greenbelt or wherever. But it's important not to feel too isolated and cut off, because there are lots of people going through the same thing.

FURTHER RESOURCES AND READING

Spiritual direction

Spiritual directors often work with people on a one-to-one basis to reflect with that person on their spiritual journey and to suggest particular resources or approaches that may be helpful for them. Spiritual direction can be particularly useful if you are trying to make sense of what is happening in your own personal spiritual development, or if you would like to explore parts of the Christian tradition or approaches to prayer that are quite new to you.

Spiritual direction can be offered simply through one-to-one meetings in your local area but can also be offered in the context of residential retreats held by various centres across the country. If you are trying to find a spiritual director or find a suitable place for you to have a retreat, then an excellent set of resources is provided by the Retreat Association. Their website (www.retreats.org.uk) contains useful resources, including details of retreat centres across Britain and Ireland. If you are looking for an individual spiritual director, you can also contact the Retreat Association directly and they can put you in touch with someone who will know more about the availability of spiritual directors in your local area. Their contact address is: The Retreat Association, Central Hall, 256 Bermondsey Street, London SE1 3UJ (Tel: 020 7357 7736).

Counselling

Again, counsellors typically work with people on a one-to-one basis, though relationship and family therapy is also appropriate in particular situations. Whilst a growing number of counsellors are aware of issues of spirituality, most counsellors will primarily be concerned with helping you on an emotional or psychological level. Some people may be able to get a limited number of counselling sessions free of charge through Employee Assistance Programmes or some other work-based counselling scheme, through local voluntary organisations or through a referral by their GP. It is also possible to pay for counselling privately which can be expensive but has the advantage of allowing you the possibility of having more sessions than some of the free counselling services can offer.

The British Association for Counselling and Psychotherapy maintains a database of individual counsellors and counselling organisations in your local area. An online version of this directory of counsellors can be found at www.bacp.co.uk, or you can contact the BACP at: The British Association for Counselling and Psychotherapy, 1 Regent Place, Rugby, Warwickshire CV21 2PJ (Tel: 0870 443 5252).

If you need specialist counselling about your relationship with your spouse or partner, there is likely to be a branch of Relate in your local area. Further details on this can be obtained from: Relate, Herbert Gray College, Little Church Street, Rugby, Warwickshire CV21 3AP (Tel: 0845 456 1310, E-mail: enquiries@relate.org.uk)

Further reading

I think there are two broad types of books that people moving on from Evangelical faith might find particularly useful. Firstly, there are a range of books that explore the process of questioning Evangelical beliefs or leaving Evangelical churches. In this category I would particularly recommend the following:

Jo Ind, *Fat is a Spiritual Issue*, Continuum, 1993. This autobiographical book offers a very honest account of the process of moving on from Evangelical faith, with a particular focus on the relationship between spirituality, eating disorders and sexuality.

Alan Jamieson, *A Churchless Faith*, SPCK, 2002. This book presents a very readable summary of an extensive research project that explored why people leave Evangelical churches. Jamieson gives plenty of examples of people's feelings and experiences as church-leavers, and offers a particular model of the process that people go through when moving away from Evangelical faith.

Dave Tomlinson, *The Post-Evangelical*, Triangle, 1995. This focuses particularly on cultural trends which have challenged Evangelical thinking and explores issues of truth and biblical interpretation beyond an Evangelical approach.

Mike Riddell, *The Sacred Journey*, Lion, 2001. Not specifically about moving on from Evangelical faith, but this book contains a lot of wisdom about dealing with significant periods of transition in our lives from a post-Evangelical perspective.

Secondly, there is a wide range of books that may help you to explore new theological ideas and forms of spirituality. This is a harder range to summarise, as different people will find different writers and books helpful in this context. You might want to keep an eye out for some of these writers, though: David Adam, Henri Nouwen, Gerard W. Hughes, Jean Vanier, Bede Griffiths, Thomas Merton, Anthony de Mello, Margaret Silf, Philip Yancey, Simon Parke, Mike Riddell, Douglas Coupland, Alain de Botton, Kathy Galloway, the Barefoot Doctor, Ursula King, Robert Beckford and Paul Tillich. This is a pretty eclectic mix and just some suggestions of people to look out for but ultimately you'll probably find it most useful to follow your nose and see what interests and inspires you.

It is worth noting, though, that there are some significant shifts in Evangelical theology as well, with some people talking about 'postconservative Evangelical theology.' A summary of this new theological trend is given in generally accessible terms in Millard Erickson, *The Evangelical Left*, Paternoster Press. 1997. Even if you don't agree with Erickson's evaluation of this movement, if you are more interested in academic theology then it will give you some ideas of other writers that you might want to follow up on.

194842UK00004B/12/P

UKOW040733220612
Milton Keynes UK
Lightning Source UK Ltd.

9 780232 525052